A CELEBRATION OF RHYME

Edited by

Steve Twelvetree

First published in Great Britain in 2000 by
TRIUMPH HOUSE
Remus House,
Coltsfoot Drive,
Peterborough, PE2 9JX
Telephone (01733) 898102

All Rights Reserved

Copyright Contributors 2000

HB ISBN 1 86161 823 9
SB ISBN 1 86161 828 X

FOREWORD

Since the first blossoming movement of contemporary verse many people have turned their back on the purest form; of poems that rhyme, and scan easily on the untrained eye. Not only has this forced many of the traditionalists to take a back bench in their pursuit of poetic fame, but many of its would-be followers have been driven away by the complexity of the modern style.

We asked our poets to challenge the modern movement and help us to compile an ultimate collection of traditional rhyming verse. So why not read on to share the true enjoyment of poetry - planting the rhyming style firmly back at its roots.

The themes inside range from poems about seasons, pets and summer holidays to odes and dedications to friends and families. This anthology brings the fun of rhyming poetry back for good and will hopefully entertain for years to come.

Steve Twelvetree
Editor

CONTENTS

Seasons Of Life	Jennifer Stella Smeed	1
What Is A Poem?	Cecilia Skudder	2
Meadows Reflections	Brian Beveridge	3
The Day I Brought My Pet Alligator To School	Lucy Porter	4
Creative Writing	Judy Smith	6
Sanctuary	Brenda D Wymer	7
The Boy Soldier	Olive Woodhouse	8
On The Take	Ken Price	9
Bampa Rees	Helen Rees-Smith	10
I Wonder	Margaret Gurney	11
Wind And Rain	Neil A Moran	12
Exile	L A Churchill	13
Parents	Sharon Smith	14
The Lee Marshes (Edmonton)	Peter Coakley	15
Busy Bee	S Brewer	16
Summertime	Cedric Anthony Thrupp	17
On Our Holiday	Trudie Sullivan	18
What Is Love?	Don Woods	19
What We Were Told	Nancy Queate	20
Autumn	Sandra Botwright	21
A Wet Journey	Denise Marriott	22
Autumn	Margaret B Baguley	23
Seasons' Greetings	Jocelyn Lander	24
Untimely Rhyme(ly)	N M Chisholm	25
Anything However Small	Mildred F Barney	26
Thoughts From An Old Woman . . .	Maggie Tate	27
The Colours Of Love	Catherine Flint	28
Harriet	Rita M Arksey	29
Crossroads	Frank Lee	30
Our English Summer	Sue Cox	31
Blue Maxi	M Eyre	32
In Paraguay	Linda Lawrence	33
The Diet	Mary Traynor	34
Percy The Personal Computer	Judith S Ruddy	35

Shares Of Pears, Pairs Of Shears	Derrick Mould	36
You Randy Old Sod	D Turberfield	37
Just Have Another Little Drag	Peggy Wright	38
The Thin End Of The Veg (Give Peas A Chance)	Matthew Shore	39
Diary Of A Nomody	Norman Ford	40
Teenage Fight	Susan Woodcock	41
Sticky Buns	Kerry Lee	42
Cyclops	June Williams	43
Reflection	Betty Nevell	44
You Thought You'd Got Away With It	John Seddon	45
Doggy Dirt Ditty	Val Baker	46
The Scots	Ethel Thomson	47
Who Am I?	WJFH	48
Birthday Card To A Seafarer And Salmon Smoker	George Theodore Harrison	50
Waiting	Hannah Yates	51
Communication	A J Spencer	52
Rhyme Time	Catherine Craft	53
Farewell To Summer	Millicent Hewitt	54
A Public Convenience	Howard Hubbard	55
From Gatwick To Gosau	David Varley	56
Van Gogh	Carol Wilkins	57
Think	Basil L Reed	58
One Spot	S Mullinger	59
What Yellow Brick Road?	Gail Walker	60
The Creeper	Keith Wilson	61
Danielle	Rob Passmore	62
Applause	Jill K Gilbert	63
What Is A Poet?	Reg Morris	64
Leaving Friends	Helena Sheridan	65
Time To Leave	Bill Hook	66
National Health 2000	Winnifred-Edith Ross	67
The Mystery Of Life	Rita Dilks	68
When	Angela Pritchard	69
The Joy Of Grandchildren	Mary Webber	70
New Day	Patricia Rose Thompson	71

The New, New Millennium	Geoffrey Garoghan	72
A Trip To The Seaside (1927)	Grace Woods	73
Destiny	Dan Pugh	74
Consternation In The Garden	Joan Thompson	75
Village Hop	Ron Dean	76
A Dog's Thoughts	Ernest Myers	77
A Cool Summer Breeze	Rajeev Bhargava	78
Ladder Of Recovery	Stephen Martin	79
Alas! Poor Silas	Sandy Chambers	80
Mother's Shopping Trolley	Pat Weeks Goodridge	81
The Longing	Laura Duncan	82
A Change Of Luck?	Paul Sanders	83
Canine-Mares	Peter Asher	84
The Pattern Of Tie-In Effete	Andrew Buchanan	85
Ode From A Chauvinist	Claire Bradford	86
The Hat - From Japan	Norman H McGlasham	87
Our Old House	Betty Glanville	88
Football Crazy	Edith Pilkington	89
Forces Favourite	K Cox	90
Beneath The Whisper	Jean Phillips	92
Life Must Go On	M A Shipp Yule	93
Megan's First Communion	Jill Dryden	94
Weekend Break	Patricia Mullins	95
Raggedy Rhubarb	Thomas J Baker	96
You're The Cat's Whiskers	Stuart Delvin	97
Vietnam Poem	Paul Wilkins	98
Table	Helen Minazza-Sturt	99
Eulogy For Diana	G Nicklin	100
Summertime Blues	E Crowhurst	101
Winters Of Yesterday	Sharon Salt	102
And Let The World Keep Turning	Clare Meadmore	103
Don't	Jean Paisley	104
The Meeting	Robert G Goodman	105
The Fire Of Love	Helen Mitchelhill	106
Always	Marion McGarrigle	107
Rain	Suie Nettle	108
Troubles To Pearls	Judith Thomas	109
Another Place - Scamp's	Ina Harrington	110

Title	Author	Page
His First Job	Paff-Pafford	111
Twenty-Two Lines	A B Lawson	112
Out Of Town	Iris Reeves	113
Kissed By A Star	Jean Mackenzie	114
State Of Being	Rosina Winiarski	115
Sing Unto The Lord	A E Turner	116
The Wayward Wind	Ivy Cawood	117
Leftover	Rosetta Stone	118
Our Dogs	Norah Bennett	119
Florida's Nature Coast	Elizabeth Hunter	120
The House	Dorothy Steadman	121
The Little Fox	Nicky Young	122
On The Beach	Louie Carr	124
White Horse Of Andalusia	Peter Gillott	125
Christmas Eve	Jane Carter	126
Bramley Court	Maureen Williams	127
The Kiss	Betty Puddefoot	128
Merry Dance	Fritzi Newlands-Du'Barry	129
Wellhouse Cottage	Josephine Grinham	130
Last Love	Joan Gordon	131
Life's Maze	Christa Todd	132
Winter Trees	Jean Wharldall	133
A Villanelle To Dawn	Hywel Davies	134
Why Poetry Is Such Fun?	O A Daley	135
The Fisher's Of London	Colin Allsop	136
Rhyme On	Danny Coleman	137
Moment Of Truth	Eileen Greenwood Sadler	138
We Love You Mandy	Karen Grover	139
Impressions	June Lane	140
The Pink Toothbrush	G E Tate	141
Blue Eyes	Jacqueline Taylor	142
Muse Blues	Brenda Söhngen	143
The Real Fairy Tale	Brenda Jane Williams	144
Happy Days	L Liggett	145
Angel	A P Starling	146
My Dad	Isobel Campbell	147
Rain	Andrew Dickson	148
My Dream Boy	Louise Collins	149

The Denim Angel	Charlotte Lythgoe	150
Mummy's Day Out	Sandra Stoner Mitchell	151
Not All Tooth Fairies Just Want Your Teeth	J Drake	152
Missing Out	Maureen Irving	153
Wonderful Hans	Vere Collins	154
Being A Fan	P Brady	155
Yum Yum Treat Land	David Watson	156

SEASONS OF LIFE

Spring and summer come and go
As the tides that ebb and flow.
First the crocus, then the swift,
Joys that make the spirit lift.

Boats rock gently on the sea
Tied to rings sunk in the quay.
Waves slap peacefully on the hull
While on the prow - a sleeping gull.

Now autumn mists swirl through the dawn
And dewdropped tendrils clothe the lawn.
The swallows soon another sky will grace
While harvest moon shines down her golden face.

The robin sings his bitter sweet lament
For fledglings nurtured, now on journeys sent.
Sunset clouds of pink and amber skies,
Scent of evening primrose on the air doth rise.

The light is fading into night
Soon the street lamps will alight.
Cars swish by on rain-soaked tarmac roads,
Hurrying home to reach their warm abodes.

Soon clocks will change to winter times
And dreams will be of warmer climes.
Embroidered webs will sparkle white
When touched with frosted fingers light.

Then for the birth we will rejoice
Loud anthems sing in one great voice.
As thanks we give to God on high
Who sent His Son for us to die.

Jennifer Stella Smeed

WHAT IS A POEM?

What is a poem?
A chance to write a poem, that well and truly rhymes,
with phrases that have meaning, and words that scan the lines!
These days it seems that poems must surely not make sense,
so every thinking person, thinks themselves a little dense!
Anglo-Saxon words are expected on each page.
Expressions want the reader to explode in deepest rage.
To really be so modern, it should be rude or very crude.
Toilet humour is much sported, all the better if it's lewd!
And surely it's more clever not to rhyme a word,
It's intellectual and clear thinking, or is it just absurd?

That's not my way of writing, I want the readers to feel good,
to realise their troubles are clearly understood.
I want to show I care, that I pray for them in pain.
That Jesus Christ our God, loves them all the same.
That hope is always there, the light within our reach.
This truth our Jesus says, we must all each other teach.
No matter what we are, or how we may offend,
His unconditional love, will never ever end.
All we have to do, is to seek His mercy now,
and He'll forgive us all - His promise, yes - His vow.
So abandon all cruel words that hurt and cause dismay.
Let poetry show love, not hatred and decay.
For in the written word, could be hope or just despair.
There's beauty in this world, which all of us should share.

Cecilia Skudder

MEADOWS REFLECTIONS

The street lights shine in puddles deep,
The trees are bare, the swings in keep.
The rain falls, lancing from the sky,
The wind brings water to the eye.
The clouds reflect a golden glow -
The City's lights far, far below.
The church's steeple blindly seeks
The stars above the clouds flushed cheeks.
The traffic's hum is muted, stark,
Yet all is peaceful in the park.

The benches stand so cold and bare;
The castle preens - high in the air.
The railings march in serried ranks;
The cars are parked by paths and banks;
The tennis courts are still and lost;
The grass is white with morning frost;
The bowling green is vacant, free;
The putting greens loom endlessly;
The houses close are quiet, dark,
And all is peaceful in the park.

Brian Beveridge

THE DAY I BROUGHT MY PET ALLIGATOR TO SCHOOL

It is now against the rule
To bring a pet alligator to school.
It was Friday; our class pet day
In the sunny month of May.
My uncle (a zoo-keeper) let me rent
A croc - that's this week's pocket money spent!
What a time I had leading to school
The massive snappy emerald jewel.
I kept him on the tight metal chain
As he snapped and snapped again and again.
When we got into the school playground
Curious people made a crowd.
Croc narrowly missed biting Lizzie on the wrist,
However, he managed to give it a sharp twist!
As the bell gave an ear-shattering sound,
The teachers walked into the playground.
The Headmaster was not pleased,
He thought that my croc just *might* have fleas!
So he locked Mr Croc
In the store-room choc-a-bloc!
In the morning, the lesson went fine,
T'was in the afternoon, that croc of mine,
Bit a hole clear through the door
And headed for the second floor.
His snappy voice could clearly be heard,
His scratchy claws like a thunder bird.
He ambled through my math's class door,
And woke up those who had begun to snore.
That's when his false teeth came out,
And every person gave a scream or a shout.
Look! The croc! He's got false choppers!
His real teeth must have come a cropper!
My croc looked very ashamed,
Evidently it was the dentist he blamed!

When the class has stopped laughing eventually,
I looked at the clock - it was nearly time for tea!
So we rushed out, the croc and I,
And I recall that horrible day with a sigh
So *that's* why there is now a rule
Not to bring alligators to school.

Lucy Porter (10)

CREATIVE WRITING

What words can I say
That will help to convey
Why I came.
Is it fame that I seek
Am I vain, am I weak?
Who can tell why the hell
I decided to write
Am I quite what I seem
Do I still have a dream
Or a need to achieve
Or a web I can weave
To enchant those who read
To inspire those who lead.
A desire for text
One word leads to the next
Until maybe a story
Will lead me to glory
And the works of my hand
Will encompass the land.
Waterstones will compete
For my works, all complete
Photo shoots, and book signing
Poet Laureate resigning.
Yes, dream on, happy heart
Write things down, make a start
Read them out, with a shout,
Don't be shy, you must try
To reveal what's inside
Never stutter and hide
Just believe in yourself
Till your name's on the shelf!

Judy Smith

SANCTUARY

My garden in the summer
Is the place that I like best.
Away from all life's hassles,
Where I toil, then sit and rest.

Outside, the world's so busy -
Rushing people, traffic, noise.
But in my garden it is quiet
And peaceful, full of joys.

The perfumes of the roses,
And the honeysuckle sweet,
Then after rain, the lavender,
Are really such a treat.

Sweet birdsong, like no other,
Is pure music to the soul.
As the blackbirds, thrushes, robins,
Sparrows, tits, all play a role.

Such brightly coloured borders
Bring the bees from miles around,
Whilst the squirrels and the woodpecker
Feed quietly on the ground.

Short crazy-paving pathways,
With a seat beneath the tree,
Provide a perfect sanctuary
When friends call in for tea.

My summer garden I declare
A most delightful place
To bond with nature, and escape
Our life's increasing pace.

Brenda D Wymer

The Boy Soldier

Sleep on warrior, no more the bugles sound
for you or your comrades who lie buried in the ground
you'll hear no more the battle cries or thunder of the gun
so sleep in peace brave soldier, for you the battle's done.

Come fight for queen and country you answered to the call
you could not know that you would be among the first to fall
with pride you donned your uniform and marched into the fray
a fine young lad who would not live to see another day.

Some mother many miles away her bitter tears will run
she will not see her lad again, her darling only son
for seventeen years she nurtured him as only a mother can
sadly she saw him go for he wanted to be a man.

What solace can one offer to all those left behind
lives permanently blighted no ease their heart can find
what for the pain of childbirth and agonies of loss
when all that's left are memories and a little wooden cross.

Olive Woodhouse

ON THE TAKE

Everybody's on the take,
what more can I say.
Everybody's on the make,
'grabbing' night and day.
Just remember this,
a fact we all must know,
in the end we'll reap,
exactly what we sow.

Everybody's on the take,
grabbing what they can.
Everybody's on the make,
holding out their hand.
Give me, give me, give me,
is the religion of the day.
Everybody's on the take,
what more can I say.

Ken Price

BAMPA REES

My grandfather I call bampa or bamps,
I think that sounds much better than gramps.
Bampa is young and fighting fit,
Not at all old or wrinkly a bit!
He's up like a lark for his Shredded Wheat,
Which is something he really loves to eat.
Then he's out in the garden tending his plants,
Or mixing Jeyes Fluid to kill all the ants.
His garden is like a magical retreat,
His flowers and veg no one can beat.
Yet he says that he hates it and finds it a chore,
But I'm sure without it, life would be a bore.
He's always smiling and happy for me,
He's my someone special and will always be.

Helen Rees-Smith

I Wonder

I wonder why the sky is blue
Why are lines straight and true
I wonder why the grass is green
And why dragons are never seen
I wonder why the world is round
And why islands are water-bound
I wonder why cars have wheels
And only human beings heels
I wonder why, I wonder why

I wonder why apes upright walk
And why only humans talk
I wonder why the night is dark
And why Noah built his ark
I wonder why trains go so fast
And if today will be my last
I wonder why we have to breathe
And what makes the earth heave
I wonder why, I wonder why.

Margaret Gurney

WIND AND RAIN

'Tis bleak this day of wind and rain
Of scudding clouds and inner pain.
'Tis bleak as well the future to
What e'er direction now I view.

Grey skies ahead and little joy
As emptiness doth now employ
My thoughts once bright and full of hope
Be as my spirit dashed and broke.

Broken too much kinship tie
As former bonds seem as to die.
Relationship no longer strong
Adds yet the more to what is wrong.

Where to now and how to fill
The future bleak as from a hill
I see no road that leadeth on
'Cept one that says all hope is gone.

Emptiness lies all around.
A stagnant pool upon the ground.
No freshness to disperse the pain
Upon this day of wind and rain.

Neil A Moran

EXILE

He hears the mermaid voices calling
'Give your hand, this way, hold me!
You promised, promised . . . marry, marry,
Stay now, no more to cross the sea'

Listen! The Lorelei is singing
'Can escape, this place, come here!
We're waiting, waiting . . . danger, danger,
sail close, your brave heart knows no fear.'

At night the Sirens sweetly tempting
'Dreams deceive, not true, not real!'
He lived there, loved there . . . this time, in time,
Anchored, his torn sleep does not heal.

L A Churchill

PARENTS

As parents
we need to make time
for storytime
for playtime
talking and listening time
bathtime is wash and fun time
for relax and rest and sleep time.
But most of all our children need
caring and loving all the time.

Sharon Smith

THE LEE MARSHES (EDMONTON)

Once lush meadows spread to the water's edge
of the meandering River Lee.
Once pure water flowed within,
And Charles Lamb walked its banks so green,
And for solace to its meadows once did go.
But that was a century or more ago.
Now black smoke billows from grey chimneys tall.
Concrete and factories have smothered all.
Whilst on the rest of vacant ground,
Rubbish tipped and domestic garbage scattered all around.
Amongst rusted tin cans, old cars discarded,
Brown and red empty hulks kissed by the wind.
Nature tries to conquer all and sparsely covers.
Fertile patches with bracken weed and twitch grasses.
Then I saw him, a small boy dressed in blue.
Dirtied denims, shirt of doubtful hue.
He was but six years of age.
In his hand he held a battered cage.
Once a shiny home for its bird owner proud,
Now just a twisted corroded rusty red.
He saw me not and in his imagination played.
On his fingers perched an invisible bird.
To it he spoke and gathered food.
Only he could see its plumage coloured.
With the sight that only a child could know.
I saw him wave goodbye to his feathered friend.
As in his mercy, he let it fly away . . .

Peter Coakley

BUSY BEE

So busy is the honeybee
That goes from flower to flower
So patiently collecting nectar
Hour after hour
So striking is the contrast
Of stripes upon his back
The brightness of the gold
The darkness of the black
So persistent is the buzz
Of the clever honeybee
And so sweet the taste of honey
That he makes for you and me

S Brewer

SUMMERTIME

As the sun shines down,
From a speedwell sky,
A sirocco blows,
Trees give a gentle sigh.

As the leaves softly rustle,
On the laden bough,
The heatwaves rise,
From the earth below.

Some birds on the wing,
Some darting back and fro,
Their pleasant twitterings,
Making up their own concerto.

With flowers in full bloom,
Each, emitting its own aromatic scent,
Their colours contrasting,
With decorative magnificence.

The cattle wander aimlessly,
Constantly at chew,
With their tails ever flicking
Away a fly or two.

The crops are nearly ready,
For the reaper to come,
We'll soon see the end,
Of this year's summer sun.

Cedric Anthony Thrupp

ON OUR HOLIDAY

The sun shines brightly over the sea,
It shines down on you,
It shines down on me.
Then the sun it goes away,
It's time to go for tea,
On our holiday.

We go walking over the hill,
The wind has stopped, it's very still,
See the lighthouse, light a-flashing,
On the rocks the sea's a-splashing.

Lots of boats out at sea,
We see them from the window
As we eat our tea.
The sun has gone,
We now have rain,
See it dripping down the windowpane.

Over the hill we see rabbits hopping,
We stay to watch,
Then go shopping.
Lots of presents we have to buy,
Oh look at that black cloud in the sky.

Down comes the rain once more,
But we're climbing in the bus's door.
In the town the bus will stop,
Then we will shop till we drop.
We all enjoy our stay,
Here, on our holiday.

Trudie Sullivan

WHAT IS LOVE?

What is love
If not the feeling that all is now secure
Such is love that has the power
To shape our lives for evermore
It can build and then destroy
As lovers' feelings it will mould
And make a glance from one who loves you
Worth more than the whole world's gold

Love is beauty, love is hunger
Love is pain, love is greed
Love is all the mixed emotions
On which mankind's soul must feed
Love is the driving force
When man or woman seeks a mate
Yet that same love has a line drawn
A line which crossed soon turns to hate

So choose wisely in your search for love
As the ideal mate you seek
Do not let your eyes be blinded
Consider your words before you speak
Rash promises and decisions made
Pledged in oath to God above
Can be regretted all through future life
Although made in the name of love

Don Woods

WHAT WE WERE TOLD

As time goes by, and we grow old,
We look back on bygone days,
And often think of what we were told
In so many different ways.

Our parents told us what was wrong and right,
As they nurtured us in their own way,
Then we always were given a hug so tight,
As we faced up to each new day.

Our school teachers, taught us to read and write,
And told us how to count,
At times we never seemed too bright,
But their teaching encouraged us to surmount.

We then got employment, and had a boss,
Who told us what to do,
Then we all had a very good cause
To say 'I will prove my worth to you.'

Then as we grew older, we fell in love,
We told each other, 'I love you,'
Then we got God's blessing from above,
When we answered to our vows, 'I do.'

We all have come through our life,
And we have been told to love one another,
We hope there will be no strife,
As we endeavour to help each other.

Nancy Queate

AUTUMN

I stand and stare as I watch the leaves fall
From the trees that stand so tall
The changing colours make me sad
Almost as if the summer's gone bad

The streets are wet with pouring rain
I hate umbrellas, they're such a pain
The wind blows my one inside out
I know it will break, without a doubt

I stand and shiver in the cold
And feel that I am growing old
I'm going now to find some heat
A glowing fire you cannot beat

Sandra Botwright

A Wet Journey

Motorway bridges, like dinosaurs grazing,
Seen through the mist of the rain that's hazing.
Spray thrown up by passing cars,
Makes headlights twinkle, like evening stars.
I know we really need the rain,
But when you're travelling, it's such a pain.
Windscreen wipers, madly waving,
Certain motorists, misbehaving.
Dark horizons, leaden skies,
Lowering clouds, and aching eyes.
Everyone seems to be in a hurry,
With dismal faces, filled with worry.
Just as you think it's all rather frightening,
You look ahead, and the skies are lightening.
The drizzling rain begins to ease,
And wispy clouds, soon start to tease.
With luck, the sun now soon will shine,
He'll dry the roads, and the day will be fine.
Then travelling becomes a joy once more,
And we're happier than we were before.
With blue skies above, and a smiling sun,
Now our journey can be fun.

Denise Marriott

Autumn

When asters flower in the garden beds,
And ragwort blooms in the lane,
When leaves are strewn by the gusty winds
It's autumn once again.
When thistledown on a gentle breeze
Comes slowly drifting by,
And the golden glow of the harvest moon
Lights up the evening sky.
When swifts and swallow leave our shores
To fly to warmer climes,
The air takes on a frosty chill
And louder sound the chimes
Of the clock in the ivy-covered tower
And stars much earlier peep,
When bats who once in twilight flew
Prepare for winter sleep.
When in the woods upon the hill
The trees are red and gold,
And spangled webs of spiders small
Show up in dewy cold.
When smoke wreathes blue from chimney stacks,
And hazy is the sun,
We welcome autumn once again
As countless seasons run.

Margaret B Baguley

SEASONS' GREETINGS

Greetings from spring - a time of new life
And new growth, as the sun warms the air.
The season comes alive with the wonders of nature,
New sights and new sounds everywhere.

Greetings from summer - Mother Nature at her best.
A time to enjoy the great outdoors.
Leisure time, carnival time, holidays and fun days,
As the magic of summer round us soars.

Greetings from autumn, a time for slowing down,
As plants start to wither and leaves start to fall.
A time for Thanksgiving as our crops are finally gathered.
A colourful season, enjoyed by us all.

Greetings from winter, a season of contrasts.
Rain and gales, snow and ice, with spells of warm sun.
Bright moonshine enhances our white wonderlands,
Winter sports and festivities add to the fun.

Our ever-changing seasons give us pleasures manifold.
Yes, the wonders of nature are a joy to behold.

Jocelyn Lander

UNTIMELY RHYME(LY)

The demands of versifying
        know no mercy (fying)
Generally for pleasing poetry
        the words should flow (etry)
Though an occasional caesura,
        rightly placed, is a pleasure (a)
Make it understandable
        to the 'ordinary man' (dable)
Treat with kindness
        the less erudite reader's mind (ness)
Verbal finesse and rhyming
        are, of course, no crime (ing)
But preserve sound grammar
        or your craft may seem a sham (mer)
Don't be so lengthy
        as to strain the poem's strength (y)
Nor be so cursory
        as to do injustice to the verse (ory)
Avoid, also, being repetitive
        - you could easily regret it (tive)
A measure of excitement
        helps to give a poem bite (ment)
And how splendid a fine crescendo
        to stir us at the end (o)

N M Chisholm

ANYTHING HOWEVER SMALL

Simplicity of Christmas
I remember years ago
Broom handle 'Merry Xmas' etched on snow
Father Xmas writing on the lawn
Not a footprint anywhere, as by magic
That message appearing Xmas morn.

Food and clothes were rationed then
Xmas trees sparsely dressed
Yet still festive spirits glowed
Excitement at its best.

Designer clothes, brand-named goods
Not on our Christmas lists
Toys, luxuries unobtainable
Tho' children then receiving gifts
Grateful 'anything however small'

Christmastime today so different
More a sort of nightmare
Advertising jingles, December
Coming sooner every year.

The reason why we celebrate obscured
Bonanza shopping, large gift-wrapped parcels
Stacked beneath the tree, ever
More extravagant, glittering, lavish
Annual spending credit card, pay later spree

Break a while, take heart, look up
Renewed unchanging splendour, simplicity
That star shining reminding
King of Kings born this day of days
Christmas, a time to give to love
Anniversary of His love, give thanks
                              in joyful praise.

Mildred F Barney

THOUGHTS FROM AN OLD WOMAN ON BEING INVITED TO A PARTY

What should I wear for this trendy affair?
They say pink and green are fit for a queen,
But yellow and green should never be seen.
Red worn with black? If one has the knack
Of mixing such hues there's nothing to lose.
Or yellow and brown for a delicate gown?
No, I don't think that's right for an elegant night.
Perhaps stick to blue, as safe dresses do?
But that can be square and I don't think I'd dare
Wear a shiny sapphire. I'd rather retire
With a run-of-the-mill gown - one that will
Hide lumps and bumps and age-telling humps.
A tent-like creation for this invitation
I guess I must find. Can't make up my mind -
Maybe I should say that I'd best stick to grey,
Or nondescript tan (not much good for élan).
Can white fit the bill? I doubt if it will -
This isn't the time, for I'm long past my prime.
It will have to be dark, though nothing too stark;
My genial host wouldn't welcome a ghost.
I'll dig out that dress (it's in rather a mess)
Which I wore for a 'do' in about ninety-two.
I'll let out some seams and by devious means
Make it more-or-less fit. If I diet a bit
It will pass in a crowd. The stuff's a bit loud
But the quality's new. It'll do.

Maggie Tate

THE COLOURS OF LOVE

Love is indigo; smart from head to toe!
Equalization! All in moderation!
Kindly; yet, firm, you are! Balanced and
Poised, you are with a feeling of elation!

Love is green, too; it can heal you!
Rejuvenating! Feels like a breath of spring!
No-one can hurt you, or, desert you! You're
Confident and keen when love is green!

Love is pink, too; warms and thrills you!
Generosity is your best quality!
People long to be in your company! You're
Prettier than you think when love is pink!

Love is yellow, too; energizes you!
Stimulating! Makes you dance and sing!
Rising early, you call a friend, or two
With their pipe and cello when love is yellow!

Love is blue, too; it can soothe you!
Sweet consolation and well-earned relaxation!
Peaceful skies above! Stress-free dreams of love
And life agrees with you when love is blue!

Love is silver, too; unravels every clue!
Congratulations and happy celebrations!
You have done your best and you've passed the test!
So, joyful exclamations and salutations!

Catherine Flint

HARRIET

She is the other female in my dear husband's life,
Thankfully of her I can say, I'm not the jealous wife.
Cream with special dark brown points and lovely big blue eyes,
That look at you so trustingly, they never tell you lies.
She is comical and funny, a hooligan at times,
But then she can be haughty, stuck up and quite sublime.
A feline queen to us she is an absolute delight,
We never will stop wondering at such a beautiful sight.
Of course she is a Siamese cat, the likes we've never met,
No other name would suit her best, but *'our Harriet'*.

Rita M Arksey

CROSSROADS

Why did the chicken cross the road?
That's a question that's been asked for years.
And that was in the days when crossing the road
Didn't really hold any fears.
Today if a chicken should cross the road,
He'd really be quite mad.
Because he'd probably end up dead
And that would be very sad.
Sad for all his family, and all his kith and kin,
They'd be reduced to poverty
Because of the state he's in.
So, chickens of the world, unite,
And listen to my plea,
Cross the road no longer and in safety you will be.

Frank Lee

OUR ENGLISH SUMMER

We have great expectations of summer!
It rarely lives up to its name.
Our hopes and our dreams
Of romantic scenes
Are extinguished by rain or by thunder.

We imagine a stroll in the country,
A doze in deck chairs by the sea.
Heat, flies, wasps and sand-fleas
Spoil picnics and cream teas!
And day-trippers travel home weary.

At best we look like boiled lobsters.
Our sunburn is scratchy and raw.
Old city gents
Don ridiculous pants
Exposing thin legs and bare paunches.

The promenade's covered in litter.
Crowds queue for fast food and some shelter.
Babes grizzle in heat.
Pavements burns 'neath our feet
And the burgers and onions smell bitter.

Spoiled children's faces grow sore
With candyfloss, lollies galore.
Dogs pant in cars,
Music blares out in bars,
The fairground attracts even more.

Girls wear nylon macs and long faces,
Amusement arcades draw them in.
The telly shows tennis
And cricket's a menace,
Fall brings a return to our senses.

Sue Cox

BLUE MAXI

I have a little dog
Her name is Blue Maxi
When she goes for walks
She always goes by taxi.
I take her to the park where she does a poo
But be careful not to tread in it
And get it on your shoe.
She's always barking at the birds
Looking high up in the sky
But sometimes there's nothing there
It makes me wonder why.
One day she was running round
But went a bit too far
It was all over in a second
She was knocked down by a car.
Now she's up in heaven
High up in the sky
Barking at all the angels
Now I know why.

M Eyre

IN PARAGUAY

In Asunción, went to a shop,
Loo paper for to find,
It was for me essential,
Shopkeeper very kind.

He stood behind the counter,
His store was just a shack,
Sparse wooden shelves, dirt at his feet,
Small child behind his back.

He asked me if I wanted,
'¿Regular, superior?'
Experience had taught me,
I paid a little more.

He placed the roll into my hand,
I paid for it and left,
Went to my room and took it out,
Unfolded it, bereft.

Grey crêpe paper, full of holes,
Hung before my eyes,
I rolled it out along the floor,
The whole street heard my cries.

If this was the superior,
What was the other like?
If even more inferior,
For sure, I'd eat my bike!

Linda Lawrence

THE DIET

My skirt won't fit, the buttons pop on blouses I once wore.
I must go on a diet
To lose a stone or more.
So I've been really good today, I've hardly ate a thing
When I was watching telly, I only had one doughnut ring.

Then I had a fruit scone, *but*, instead of butter, I used jam.
I only had a few chips, with my two fried eggs and ham.
And I only had three sugars
In my fourteenth cup of tea.
So I'm really disappointed, this diet didn't work for me.

Mary Traynor

Percy The Personal Computer

It was logic to call me Percy, I am a new PC,
I sit at my work station, plugged in and quite pristine.
With display screen and printer, and hard disc ready to byte,
I am prepared for anything, from memory to world website.
Often my cursor twitches, when someone grabs my mouse,
And searches round the menu, for a title to expound.
Could it be a spreadsheet, or vital dates programmed,
perhaps a business letter, or something just randomed.
My microchip is very small, it's all I need to feed me,
Unless by chance a virus strikes, then I'm useless Percy PC.
Once you have acquired the knack, com. literate to a T,
It's amazing how much data can be stored inside of me.
Even on a floppy disc the information mounts,
When you press another key, the printer prints it out.
When you're on the network, Internet, or world-wide web,
There's no end of info you can cram inside your head.
History, geography, languages and maths,
Virtual reality, displays, designs and graphs.
So don't let me just sit here waiting to be used,
Put something into database, to view on VDUs.

Judith S Ruddy

SHARES OF PEARS, PAIRS OF SHEARS

The fair is here, just near the Square,
Now care to hear what they have there?
A bear, a mare, a hare, a deer,
A tent with beer and maid near bare.

And near the fair there is a seer,
A cheery kind of dear, whose hair
Is queer, and if you glare it's clear
Her hair is fair right near the rear.

Now please don't jeer, but on the pier
I've an idea there's a rare pair
Of chairs veneer, no wear or tear,
And other gear just nearby here.

The fare to there (the pier) is dear,
Though near to here, but I do hear
That they do care about high fares;
Dare they cut theirs and risk careers?

Let's cheer the mayor whose name is Claire,
Who found a fox's den or lair,
This was last year, near Pear Tree Square,
And near the lair there was a snare.

Those glares and tares and wheres and sears,
Ears, veers, flares, wares and smears and leers,
And other 'eers' I've missed, I swear,
I fear I've no more flair to air.

Derrick Mould

YOU RANDY OLD SOD
(Translated: octogenarian modus operandi)

As a means of communication
        In respect of old age and recall,
I carry a small silver whistle
        To cater for short, fat or tall,
Passing females of promising age group
        Appearing in my field of view
When I gladly respond to its usage,
        With a grin or an odd wink or two.

It's one pleasure I've almost forgotten.
        When young, I vibrated with glee,
But today's strain of old rigor mortis,
        Knock the hell out of what used to be.
So a pleasure delicious in nature,
        Orgasmic . . . delightful, 'tis true,
Generates most thankful assistance,
        This old whistle,
                When blown,
                      Might give you!

So, living in hopes almost daily,
        I pray to the powers up above,
To put the best pea in my whistle,
        For affairs of the heart and of love.

D Turberfield

JUST HAVE ANOTHER LITTLE DRAG

Lizzie crept behind the shed
        To have a crafty drag
She was nearly twelve and quite grown up
        But she had never smoked a fag

Her brother and a couple of pals
        Had gathered their weekend spends
A penny apiece bought Woodbine five
        A secret treat between four friends

They puffed and coughed and all turned green
        A sadder sight you have never seen
As they all made a mad dash
        To the lavvy

The years have rolled on
        And Lizzie's friends - they're all dead and gone
Now she sits by her window
        Still puffing but sadly alone

Her hair has turned grey, her face looks grey too
        She knows the best thing she ought to do
Throw those coughing sticks
        Straight down the loo

'Ambulance please' she gasped down the phone,
        'I cannot breathe and I'm scared on my own.'
At last it arrived but five minutes too late
        Poor old Lizzie was already standing at St Peter's gate

Frantically trying to stamp out her last dog-end
        On a feathery cloud!

Peggy Wright

THE THIN END OF THE VEG (GIVE PEAS A CHANCE)

Linda watches as I eat my last sausage
As I swallow my conscience, as I swallow my guilt
But there's children dying as my bacon's frying
So there's no point crying over blood that's spilt

I'm a proper meat-eater
I've abandoned all veg
Linda won't make me teeter
As I stand on this ledge

But I still see Linda wave her fishless finger
And I choke on my dinner, I choke on my sin
So I rid my kitchen of its streaky bacon
And I find salvation in a chickenless wing

Now my body's a temple
Where I go to pray
And I dine upon lentils
And tofu and hay

But now I can't help thinking 'bout the milk I'm drinking
Are the cows all shrinking as I swallow their milk?
And I wonder whether my uppers are leather
And how many feathers were plucked for my quilt

Am I going quite mental?
My pulse is low
I'm becoming a lentil
A compulsive loaf

Now my family's disowned me and my friends never phone me
But how can I feel lonely when Linda's my chum?
And I'm happy completely being pallid and weakly
Till the bacon cries 'Eat me!' and I finally succumb

Matthew Shore

DIARY OF A NOMODY

When I start to write a verse, whatever theme my pen is on,
I try to follow geniuses like Chaucer, Keats and Tennyson,
I study all their expertise, but am told it's inadvisable
For skills with rhyme and lines that scan, are now not recognisable.

The modern poet, I am warned, is doomed to death and failure
If he clutters up the Muse's path with useless paraphernalia
Like capitals and sentences and verses systematical,
Or pays too much attention to outmoded rules grammatical.

That I should suffer from this ill you might term a disability,
And success, unless I find a cure, is beyond all credibility.
My ways, I fear, are out-of-date, distinctly dinosaureate.
How can I ever hope to be the future Poet Laureate?

Norman Ford

TEENAGE FIGHT

My two teenage daughters fight like cat and dog
they are like chalk and cheese
and they think money grows on trees!

Our house is always noisy with loud music and slamming doors
the smell of hairspray, you almost choke
my new lipstick! Broke!
I need a rest!
But I know I will miss them dearly
when they leave the nest.

Susan Woodcock

STICKY BUNS

It was the last day of term for the youngest class,
So a party we held for each lad and each lass.
A drink, some crisps and a large sticky bun,
Then we stood back, smiled, and watched the fun
        As they ate their sticky buns.

Most started to eat their bun from the top,
Stopping only for a drink of fizzy pop.
This group could be recognised by the icing on each nose,
Although young Robert managed to get some on his toes.
        Lovely sticky buns.

The second group were those with lots of hair,
It didn't matter how they ate, it really wasn't fair.
Each mouthful involved removing a long tress,
They all ended up in a terrible mess
        And hair in their sticky buns.

The next group decided to remove the paper first,
This seemed to give them a terrific thirst.
As they grasped their beakers, they seemed to stick,
Then Kirsty was most spectacularly sick.
        She was allergic to sticky buns.

The last group just picked bits off the top of their bun
And flicked them over the table - they thought this was fun.
Then they licked their fingers one by one
And threw what was left at Carol and John.
        Missiles from sticky buns.

At last it was home time, so they stood in line,
Then trooped out to their mums and began to whine.
'We had sticky buns, that's why there's jam in my hair.'
I turned back to clear up - that was my share
        Of the sticky buns.

Kerry Lee

CYCLOPS

Sitting in the corner of the living room,
My single grey eye staring out through the gloom,
The house is so quiet and the atmosphere dead,
The family said their goodbyes and now it's off to bed,
During the day for many hours gone past,
I've given out music with a vital blast,
The words before said were both long and loud,
I can truthfully say I played to a crowd,
It seems they've all gone and the house is quiet,
Only memories left of what once was a riot,
There's no light in my eye - it is for the best,
For this very old TV is needing a rest.

June Williams

REFLECTION

I used to say,
When I was blue,
'If only I could
Be like you'

And now I am,
My constant plea
Is 'Please God turn me
Back to me!'

Betty Nevell

You Thought You'd Got Away With It

A touch of moisture on the cheek
                    a wrinkle on the brow
You bite your lips and you cannot speak
                    you keep on asking how
It's not the dog, it's not the cat
                    it's time to make amends
For quietly letting off like that
                    in front of all your friends.

John Seddon

DOGGY DIRT DITTY

When walking in our lovely town
    And doggy deposits you spot
    Please don't blame every dog owner
For we're not all an irresponsible lot!

Of course there are the lazy few
    Who can't be bothered to pick up
    That nasty pile of doggy poo
Produced by his errant pup!

For most of us are considerate
    And take the problem home,
    But then you get the other sort
Who leave their dogs to roam.

So please don't judge by the bad ones
    Or blame the dog - indeed . . .
    Don't curse or shout at the poor animal
But the clown at the *other* end of the lead!

Val Baker

THE SCOTS

Scots are spartan
They dress in tartan
Wi' kilts o' plaid
That granny made
In her Heilan hame
Flashin' dirks
Gaun tae kirks
Tae renounce the de'il
An a' his works
Suppin' Scotch in but'nbens
Then fleein' like streams
Doon the glens.

Ethel Thomson

Who Am I?

I am old yet I feel young.
I've written songs that are never sung.
My mind is often far away.
I hope tomorrow is another day.

Why? Because day and night are both the same.
My mind is strong my body lame.
The things I say may well confuse.
I never win . . . I never lose.

The game I play is full of chance.
The cards are laid I want to dance.
I join the never-ending throng.
The music plays I sing their song.

Yes! I follow while the piper plays.
The hooker works the bishop prays.
The devil laughs the singer sings.
Tomorrow promises better things.

Here I am a man half born.
Which has more beauty the rose or thorn?
My body runs on half a heart.
Which came first the horse or cart?

The pieces don't seem to fit in place.
Have I fallen from God's grace?
Can I return like the Prodigal Son?
Or just keep running as fast as I can.

If I run I daren't look back.
Tread with care don't step on a crack.
For should I fall . . . before I rise,
I must collect the booby prize.

Reader! If by chance you solve this rhyme,
You'll glimpse beyond the end of time.
And realise just who I am, and
Where and how it all began!

WJFH

Birthday Card To A Seafarer And Salmon Smoker

Smoky Joe, here we go -
        The kiln is off,
        So we will scoff.
                On this your anniversary, say.
        How does it go, for you I mean,
        On this your eightieth birthday?

Your dog on the face
        Of this card, looks grand.
        His face is happy and, not bland.
        He is looking for a bite, a kiss,
                Or a cuddle.
        After all, when he is out,
                He keeps out of trouble.

So we say to you, Joe
        'Engine room, to bridge!'
        Don't put your gifts
                In the fridge!

Some in the shell, and some, on the bone,
        Cook them all up, and enjoy
                Them at home.

Once again, Jean and I, say
        Have a lovely, happy, day.
        Your dog too.
                So we say,
                        Toodle-oo.

George Theodore Harrison

WAITING

When the earth is white and the sky is grey
It's hard to recall a summer's day
Where the swallows dart and the humming bee
Adds her dizzy song to life's melody.

(And a distant hum in a sapphire sky
As a lazy plane sees the world go by.)

Yet - it helps to know, as grey days drag by
That it won't be long till we see a sky
Picture-framed by blooms on a cherry tree.
We'll hear once more miss busy bee -
Smell fresh-mown grass and scented flowers;
Have time to while-away the hours
And bless each precious hour that we
Can tuck inside our memory.

Hannah Yates

COMMUNICATION

I drew the curtain to reveal a scene of bitter chill
Split second as bright eyes met mine, he came, my hungry bird
A sudden fluttering of wings onto the window sill
Asking me for food, more clearly than the human word

'Coming now' I said and donned my boots and coat and hat
Scraping snow away I left the pile of tasty crumbs
Watching from behind the glass there was my jealous cat
Meeting my forbidding stare, to furious rage succumbs

Thwarted there he watched the blackbird's busy yellow beak
Frustration rising as he knew his quarry out of reach
Only to our species we concede ability to speak
Not ours, but universal is the power of silent speech!

A J Spencer

RHYME TIME

What have we done in our lifetime
To all the poems which could rhyme?
It has become a trend to write
Without a shape or form, in spite
Of all the people who love rhyme.
We'll bring it back in our time.

We'll introduce rhyme into schools
We could use homonyms and rules
That every person tries their hand
To follow guidelines; join our band
Of poets who insist on rhyme.
We'll bring it back in our time.

We'll write to teachers all around
And tell them rhyming will help sound
Work for the young who cannot read.
It still fulfils a simple need
For them to guess the word in rhyme.
We'll bring it back in our time.

We'll write to college teaching staff
For whom rhyme often makes them laugh.
We'll tell them educate the young
Who'll join the rhyming ladder's rung.
They'll find that they will enjoy rhyme
We'll bring it back in our time.

We'll write to Whitehall with great skill.
We'll make them take the bitter pill
To accept that rhyme's good for all
That lack of shape or form will call
Us back to verses all in rhyme.
We'll bring it back in our time.

Catherine Craft

FAREWELL TO SUMMER

The long days of summer are over and past
a beautiful dream just beyond our grasp
a forest of trees that were once decked with green
now stand resplendent with bright golden sheen
the thrush's song silent, swallows flown away
picnics all finished, no trips round the bay.

By the fence a last rose half-heartedly sway
till the wind and the rain sweep its beauty away
the wet garden seat not a welcoming place
where you recently sat with the sun on your face
the mornings are colder there's mist in the air
to warn us that winter is coming - Beware!

The older I grow seasons seem to change fast
this summer already belongs to my past
but memories linger maybe some little thing
when we look back it will make our heart sing
farewell to summer, winter's on the way
summer will soon be a new yesterday.

Millicent Hewitt

A Public Convenience

I skip up through the alley after dropping off my wheels,
To a curious little building where great unease I feel.
I'm bombarded with echo and slimy grimy floors,
How I feel unhappy as I slither through that door!
Dripping, shining metal and soaking rock-hard floor,
Meet in grisly half-light where horrors lie in store.
We stand in line like statues with eyes fixed to the wall,
But with those strangers close to me, I can never go at all!

Posters about VD, condoms and diseases,
In this cell of murky sin is there anything that pleases?
The plumbing how it gurgles and makes a fearful din,
Soap and water both run out - there's no room in the bin.
The moral of this story reluctantly I tell,
Entering such gloomy caves is an awful living hell.
Why don't we drop a stick of bombs to make such buildings yield,
And for our own convenience - why don't we use a field?

Howard Hubbard

FROM GATWICK TO GOSAU

People crowding everywhere,
Gatwick airport, check-in time;
MasterSun assembling now
Off to Oberammergau.

Where do I go? Who do I know?
Flight delayed. Four hours to go.
I wait alone but look around
To see what labels can be found
On cases, that will indicate
Who's in the Gosau syndicate.

They're all around the lounge dispersed,
But one I see whose name is Hurst
Behind the Daily Telegraph
As silent as the Cenotaph.

Vernon's his name, composed, serene,
A welcome sight in such a scene.
Judith then, his wife, appears,
Bright and blithe, dispelling fears.

Quite soon the screens will indicate
That, though the plane is somewhat late,
We should assemble by gate eight
And end our uninspiring wait.

At Salzburg when we land it's hot.
I claim my case and find a spot
On Bruce's coach, and gaze in praise
At mountains, rivers, pastures, trees.
They raise my spirit, lift my heart
With thoughts that this is just the start
Of something God already knows
Will bless and lift me from my woes.

David Varley

VAN GOGH

I study your paintings with interest and care
I see all the flaws of your life hidden there.
A spirited legend in arts inspiration
trying to relate in rejected frustration.
The masterpiece painting you tried to create,
in nature's own splendour, in silent debate.
Ignored and belittled, your visions unshared,
a God-given talent for which nobody cared.
Your fears were unheard, your life was unwhole
despair and destruction enveloped your soul.
The need to be loved held far too much strife,
so dejected and lost, you sacrificed your life.
All too late your aptitude was shown
the insight and dreams of your gift have now grown.
A cruel twist of fate, which cut short your endeavour,
made death your awakening, immortal forever.

Carol Wilkins

THINK

Think not of things as you wish they were,
Think only of things as they really are.
Think, yes think; of the maiden with skin so fair,
Think not of her with flesh laid bare,
Nor lust after the ladies laid in bed,
Or after the street girl dressed in red.
Think only those thoughts that are pure and true,
Think only of living for the good you can do.
Think of the scientists who tried their best,
With those Accursed Atomic Tests.
To wrest from the Earth, its heart and soul,
On some far distant Pacific Atoll.
Polluting the sea, and the air we breathe,
Withering the foliage on the trees.
The Earth cries out, she's on her knees,
A prayer to God; oh, stop them please!
For stop man will, ere it's too late.
For the Lord's Grim Reaper - is at the gate.

Basil L Reed

ONE SPOT

'Only one spot' said Doctor Paul,
'Hardly noticeable at all.'
'But you're just a man' I replied,
And as I left his room I sighed.

A man just does not understand,
That spots on faces should be banned.
I will not go out anymore,
Embarrassed to be seen outdoors.

One spot has grown into many,
Losing friends, soon won't have any.
How can I meet other people,
With my face full of red pimples?

Each day pray for some improvement,
As I apply sticky ointment.
But sure affected area grows,
While my ego suffers new blow.

None can enjoy looking like this,
Treatment seems very hit or miss.
Long for the spots to disappear,
So I can say my skin is clear.

S Mullinger

WHAT YELLOW BRICK ROAD?

Remember the story of the Yellow Brick Road
That wound a path, as to Oz it flowed? . . .
Once this path lay calm in yellow gloss,
Not lost in chaos and nuclear dross.
Who remembers Dorothy and Toto, her pet,
Or their search for Oz on which they were set.
Or a lion - seeking courage so he could roar,
Or a Straw-Man - a brain so no longer a bore.
For the Tin-Man - a heart to love and be cherished,
Or just a way home before they all perished.
It all seemed so easy . . . would life was so neat!
I've trodden my path till I've corns on my feet!
I've followed the route that I was set,
I've plodded regardless but not arrived yet.
I've toiled to succeed to the end of my road
And all of my seeds were so neatly sowed.
But some get the weeds, it's the luck of the draw
Some struggle - some win, why . . . I'm not sure.
But if I don't find where my Oz is lying,
One thing - it's not for the lack of trying.
I've got the red slippers, in need of a stitch . . .
I've done well up to now in avoiding the witch.
I'm good at attracting the waif and the stray
I've got my Brasso to buff up the way.
So shine up the bricks and follow them round,
Say 'Hi' to the wizard . . . if ever he's found!

Gail Walker

THE CREEPER

A creeper once was planted,
On a cold North-facing wall,
The gardener wanted her to spread,
To cover the bricks and all.

In the weeks that followed,
She strove her best to grow,
But the sun was so unkindly
And the frost so cruel so.

Alas, one day a child at play
Broke off her slender stem,
'It's no use' she cried
'I'll never grow again.'

But she was so courageous,
A brave, hidden spirit she found
And started sending up new shoots,
Directly from the ground.

One day she got her just rewards,
For all her courage and strife,
The gardener came and transplanted her,
To start a brand-new life.

Now on a warm, South-facing wall,
Where the sun kissed her all day
And the gentle breeze caressed her,
She grew and grew away.

She grew so strong and beautiful
And when the tale is told,
Her crown of joy was autumn,
With her leaves tinged red and gold.

Keith Wilson

DANIELLE

This is the year
My girl is eleven
It doesn't seem five minutes
Since she was seven.
From the time she was born
When I was there
A small, little bundle
With not much hair.
The greatest dad
Maybe I am not
But my love for Danielle
Should not be forgot.
I've tried my best
For her at all times
I'll love her always
Because she is mine.
I'm very proud to be her dad
When we argue it makes me sad
I know deep down she's the same
But to love her always is my aim.
So Danielle, sweetheart
I write this for you
And I hope one day
You'll be proud of me too.

Love always Dad

Rob Passmore

APPLAUSE

Time to clap, I've finished now,
Don't you think I've raised a brow,
For years I've worked on the stage,
I thought I would appeal to someone's age.

Perhaps I'm too old now to cavort around,
People might think I'm a bit of a clown,
But please, I love what I do,
So leave me alone, will you.

Let me have my five minutes of fame,
I'm sure you would want to do the same.

Well time to go on stage now,
Watch if you will,
But please clap and cheer at the end,
When I take my bow and don't be still.

Jill K Gilbert

WHAT IS A POET?

Anyone who can put words down could be worthy of acclaim
Yet it will depend on the judge who may not rate it with much fame.
To keep the work original we should not follow any lead
For to develop an idea we have, is all we really need.
Famous poets through the age must have practised this to start
And to make it all so readable must be an acquired art.
To study others work could somehow stifle our ambition
So that the aim to be original may never come to that fruition.
Almost any subject can be made use of and translated into rhyme
And it can all be made interesting if we take a little time.
Maybe something happened as we went through our usual day
So we could try to record it before we put that pen away.
We might just meet a neighbour and merely ask his state of health
And find that since you last met he has gained considerable wealth.
You see I've not taken any subject and yet my pen doesn't want to stop
It shows that writing poetry can be almost like talking shop.
And so I could go on and on, as we know some people do
Until we get fed up with it, so you may now suspect a clue.
I'm going to end this writing now - I'll put my pen away
But to sum up I think anyone can write poetry so pick up
                                       your pen today.

Reg Morris

LEAVING FRIENDS

This life holds many moments
And some of them so dear,
The dusty, shadowed memories
We carry year by year,
Yet here I have a moment
And what else can I do,
But spend it thinking happily
Of all the times we knew.
Sweet things I shall remember
And sadly, when they're gone,
They too shall be a memory
That I can dwell upon.
As ripples in the ocean
And stars that fade and die,
The hardest part of meeting
Is always the 'goodbye',
Yet I'm glad that I have known you
And life has seen it fit,
That I should pass where you should pass
And linger for a bit.
For life holds many moments
And if they were compared,
Undoubtedly, the special ones,
Are moments that we've shared.

Helena Sheridan

TIME TO LEAVE

Oh Lord, do not take me in winter's gloom,
When days are short and the nights so long.
I have no wish to journey in the dark,
Nor when winds blow cold and the frost is sharp.

Lord, call me in the heat of the day,
With a preference for the month of May.
When the leaves of beech are fresh and green,
And the tall grass waves in the gentle breeze.
Or, beckon me as the corn shows ear
Bursting through in summer's dawn so clear.
At that time in my favoured seasons
I will not struggle or seek a reason.
I promise not to stumble or falter
When you summon me to lay at your altar.

Then take my spirit and scatter it far,
In woods, hills and fields and along the sea shore.
And please guard the heart of my worldly life
To lay embraced in the arms of my wife.

Bill Hook

NATIONAL HEALTH 2000

Said Nye Bevan from up in heaven
Looking down on Gordon Brown,
'What's this I see, did we not agree
The National Health Service would be free.
It wasn't meant just for the wealthy
But to make the poorer healthy.
And by doing so we would save
A lot of people from an early grave.'

'Now listen to me Mr Nye.'
Said Mr Brown looking up on high.
In 48 that would be just the tonic
But in 2000 things are really chronic.
More wards are closing every day
And nurses are on lower pay.
And it wouldn't matter how loud you holler
The waiting list doesn't get any smaller.
But I've been told by Mr Blair
To show you that we really care
And we pledge that pound for pound
We shall turn this national round.
And I hope without deception
We have found the right prescription.

So Mr Bevan up in heaven
Raised his glass to Mr Brown
As he said 'Don't let me down,
Now you've got some extra wealth.
Put it into the nation's health
Don't think about the next election
Just give us that massive injection
                           (of money).'

Winnifred-Edith Ross

THE MYSTERY OF LIFE

Learn to take what life gives out
Whether it be good or bad.
Learn to know the reasons
We feel happy, we feel sad.
Know that always no matter what
Whether we be rich or poor
Life is something wonderful
And who could ask for more.
Maybe sometimes it doesn't give out
The things we had in mind
But look towards the lessons
And the inner truth you'll find.
Yes, life is but a mystery
As our journeys we begin
Discovering keys to heaven
As we cast aside all sin.
The only thing that matters
Is that we do our very best
Life is not a mystery
It's just a Heavenly Test.

Rita Dilks

WHEN

When the whole world rushes past you,
Take a moment to show you care,
When friends find themselves in trouble,
Spend some time all their cares to share.

When love is all you have to give,
True friendship will always shine through,
When it's you that needs helping hands,
Friends will rally round to help you.

When a smile is all that matters
And a friendly word says it all,
When you're there if you are needed,
You'll be the one that's walking tall.

When you show by your example
That of greed and spite there's no need,
When following your ideals,
They're bound in the end to succeed.

Angela Pritchard

THE JOY OF GRANDCHILDREN

Grandchildren are like rays of sun
Full of warmth, love and fun.
They really brighten up each day
With little things they do and say.

Like each new flower, they gently unfold
New words, habits and joys untold.
Like each flower, they bend their heads
Then we love them - snug in their beds.

Their world is new, things to explore
A big adventure, an open door.
If we could see things through their eyes
Maybe we would be more wise.

A little patience, love and care
Will let them know we are always there.
When they are naughty and not so good
We still adore them - like only grandparents could.

Mary Webber

NEW DAY

Oh spirits of wisdom, we seek your aid,
To avoid temptation and wrongs to evade.
As through life's streams, rivers and seas we wade,
But with truth, sincerity, justice and love, our debt to the
                creator will be paid.

Our combined strengths and unity will be met with a new beguine,
Determination, God's will, love for each other will overcome and win.
Fortified, renewed, a new spiritual age is dawning,
We await with patience and trust to herald in the glorious morning.

Patricia Rose Thompson

THE NEW, NEW MILLENNIUM

Bearing in mind as I write this it's June,
There is something I'm certain will happen quite soon.
As December rolls by and two-thousand departs,
you'll hear 'here's where the *real* new millennium starts'.

There'll be business and industry ads by the score,
with *'millennium deals', special-offers'* and more.
There'll be *'special-editions'* of coins, cars and stamps,
plus a race to give birth on the first day of Jan.

And I'd sure be surprised if *that* newspaper fails,
to cash-in on the chance, to up *soaraway* sales.
And there's bound to be those who grab each chance they find,
just to prophecies *sic* doom, or the end of mankind.

I can understand them wanting to be one of the few,
who finds fame if their forecast should ever come true.
But, a flaw in their plan could present quite a blow,
if their forecast comes true, well nobody will know!

So now I'll wear the shoes of a prophet awhile,
and I'll make this prediction, though not to beguile.
When you thought the millennium fuss was all done,
just you sit tight and wait for two-thousand and one.

Geoffrey Garoghan

A TRIP TO THE SEASIDE (1927)

Come along Mother said 'It's high time you were in bed,
Tomorrow we both get the train, we are off to see the sea again.'
Hopping and skipping with delight,
Gracie went to bed for the night.

Early next morning Mother made sandwiches and fresh lemonade,
Then off they went jollily for their day next the sea.
'Have a good day' the porter cried as he helped Mother get inside.

The morning sun so brightly shone, as they happily jogged along,
Both eagerly waiting soon to reach, their destination by the beach.
The train pulled in right on time,
With a whistle and a puff at the end of the line.

'Hurry, I can hardly wait' Gracie cried going through the gate.
Mother clutching bag and sunshade, Gracie carrying a bucket and
                spade.
'There's Punch and Judy, donkeys too and ice cream for me and you.'

Mother rested in a deckchair, Gracie played without a care,
Making sandcastles on the seashore, collecting bright pebbles by
                the score,
Catching crabs and watching them run, back to the sea and out of
                the sun.

Along came the donkeys, side by side, the lady called out
'Anyone for a ride?' Mother agreed to Gracie's delight,
Then off she trotted merry and bright, along to the pier and back again,
By then it was time to catch the train.

Mother was waiting in the shade with bag all packed and bucket
                and spade.
They got to the station the train was there, luckily with two seats
                to spare.
Gracie was tired and ready for bed,
'Oh! There's a crab in my bucket Mother' she said.

Grace Woods

DESTINY

We are not called to ape the ways
Of good folk from long bygone days
Whose thoughts, or words, or startling deeds
Are writ in books, or songs, or creeds.

We are not meant to imitate
Another, nor yet subjugate
Our own essential quality -
Our individuality!

But we must take the life God gave,
And carry it beyond the grave;
And there present before His Throne
What we have made - how we have grown!

Dan Pugh

CONSTERNATION IN THE GARDEN

There's consternation in the garden
Next-door have a cat.
I know she'll not be welcome,
I'm very *sure* of that!

The blackbirds swoop and scold her,
They're making such a fuss,
She may be 'someone's darling'
But they don't like the puss.

The magpies watch and cackle,
They quite enjoy the affray,
They also cause much trouble
In their own particular way.

The robin 'tuts' and flits about,
His territory's been invaded,
He really cannot allow this,
The cat on his plot has paraded.

The wise owl sits and ponders,
He knows she's no match for him
When it comes to out manoeuvring
He knows that he will win.

The sparrows chatter 'Just fancy that!'
The garden was theirs, so they thought
The trees and bushes give shelter
Hopefully none will be caught.

Will there ever be peace in the garden again?
Not while pussy's around.
Perhaps they'll work some agreement out -
The garden for puss - *'Out Of Bounds!'*

Joan Thompson

VILLAGE HOP

They're dancing the Samba, I'll miss it this time
And stay at the bar drinking lager and lime.

The blonde in the red dress, with her mate by the door,
Jenny or June? I've seen her before.

The next is a Quickstep and this is my chance,
To push through the crowd and ask her to dance.

She smiles at me sweetly and whispers her name
And while we are dancing I do the same.

She's as light as a feather, so graceful, divine,
Where I lead she follows, this partner of mine.

Fox-trots and Rumbas to name just a few,
We dance every number till evening is through.

And now the Last Waltz, drowsy head on my chest
As I hold her tight, dare I make the request?

'Can I walk you home?' - her friend has now gone,
'It's rather a long way, I'd like you to John.'

A kiss and a cuddle, it's now getting late,
Then the final embrace as we part at the gate.

We've promised to meet again, go dancing soon,
Perhaps we're an item, me and my June?

There's four miles to trudge between me and my bed
But my young heart is leaping and I'm light in the head.

Ron Dean

A Dog's Thoughts

To walk through fields all white with snow
Following animals' tracks as to their homes they go.
To see children's faces light with delight
As they shout and scream in their snowball fight.
Walk beneath the slow, falling flakes
As a gentle wind blows, giving trees the shakes
Silence and peace are all around
When winter's snow decorates the ground.
My master walks with me
As I stop, sniff, look and want to know
What is this stuff that humans call snow?
Oh yes it's nice and soft on gentle paws
But I don't wear shoes my feet are colder than yours.

As winter's chill and snow grips the land
Myself and the children make a happy band.
Our thoughts drift back to warm summer days
Trying to ignore the winter's ways.
Try to shut from your mind the icy cold
Myself and the children don't feel it
Maybe we will, when we like you, grow old.

Ernest Myers

A Cool Summer Breeze

As I sit poised on my dark, empty chair,
I gaze out the window without any care.
They are wide open and attract me to see
Lush, green and maroon, bright petalled trees.
In deep admiration, I forget all my problems; all about me.
And as I slump back, nearly falling on my knees,
A strong gush of wind blows, a cool summer breeze.

Rajeev Bhargava

LADDER OF RECOVERY

Right now! My goals are way too high,
I must think before I try.
And ease my way towards the sky,
Pausing for the passer-by.
Not too quick and not too slow,
But take it easy as I go.
Nice and simple, that's the way!
Beginning from the loading bay.

No giant leap from here to there,
Just small steps of taking care.
There's no cause to overdo,
For patience is a true virtue.
I must crawl before I walk,
Utter sounds before I talk.
Learn the things I need to know,
Gaining knowledge as I go.

Up the ladder of recovery,
The beginnings of a new discovery.
Edging into living's ring,
Being part of everything.
It is me, for I am here,
Stepping up another gear.
I have come and I will stay,
Up the ladder and on my way,
To a brighter, happy day.

Stephen Martin

ALAS! POOR SILAS

The gentle breeze caressed his face,
He's ran his earthly race.
The years of toil are over,
No more to roam through the clover.

The clock of life but once is wound,
And earthly ties are bound.
Through morning, noon and night
And seasons dull and bright.

The golden corn grows in the field,
It's bounty yet to yield.
No more for him the bread of life,
He's left that to his wife.

His life span now expired,
No more will he be hired,
Of all, he was the best
They've laid him to his rest.

Sandy Chambers

MOTHER'S SHOPPING TROLLEY

Now that Ma is seventy-plus, we thought she needs a trolley,
Nothing posh, just practical, to help her haul her caulies.
So to the Charity Shop we went and much to our surprise,
There before the counter stood *a trolley*, bargain buy!
It looked a trifle tatty, but the frame in good repair,
So home we went to clean it up, and make it look quite fair.
Ma was quite delighted 'It's just what I can use, I'm not as
Fussy as you,' she said, 'It's clean and that will do!'
Now to the village shops she sped, best not get in her way,
She'll mow you down as look at you, it's her weekly shopping day!
She piled the trolley very high, it was a heavy load,
She should be licensed to drive that thing, and keep death off the road!
Ma flitted here and flitted there, the load got even higher,
She was tickled with her shopping spree, it filled her heart's desire.

Now, back to base the idea was, for a well-earned cup of tea,
Wot a good idea this trolley was, with it she was well-pleased!
But, on the homeward journey, Ma had clean forgot the hill,
As the trolley gathered momentum and for her *O Gawd* a spill!
The locals gasped in horror, cats and dogs fled out the way,
As Ma attached to trolley, shot past without delay!
She fought hard to halt the gadget, sparks spluttering from the wheels,
She'd gone from nought to sixty and she wasn't very thrilled!
She thought she was in orbit, first trolley-launch in space,
'What will the neighbours think,' she wailed 'I'll be a huge disgrace!'
And then, as if by magic, the trolley hit a stump,
Ma had landed on her bum, the trolley twisted junk!
'I'll never push another,' Ma was heard to say, and
'Bugger silly trolleys,' and 'Goodbye shopping days!'
The moral of this story is plain for all to see,
Never push what you can pull and buy only what you need!

Pat Weeks Goodridge

THE LONGING

I dreamed that all the world was healed
Of pain and sorrow's woes,
No more the cry of infant child
As through its life it goes.
But free of want and heartache
Takes its first faltering steps,
Toward the journey we all make
Unchartered map as yet.
There were no hurtful people who
Would cause the child to cry
The animals were peaceful too
Together they did lie.
The air was clean and scented
And full of birds of song,
To each of them was granted
To sing the whole day long
A sweet and pleasant melody
Upon the fragrant air,
No fear for anybody
But peace for all to share.

Laura Duncan

A CHANGE OF LUCK?

I look forward to tomorrow much more than yesterday,
It seems that when you've lost so much, there's not much more to say.
I lost my job last Christmas and my wife left in a fight,
My bank account is overdrawn and friends shun me on sight.
I slipped down the stairs and hurt my leg yesterday at half past nine
And after that I crashed my car into a road halt sign!
There doesn't seem to be much more which could happen to me now,
The future *must* be brighter - I've lost my way somehow.
At least I still retain my health and manage still to smile,
With luck like mine you've got to laugh, the outlook *must* be fine.
But too soon did I imagine that bad luck would change that day,
The Gods threw their dice and again I lost as a truck crashed through
                                                                                my gate.
I jumped into some bushes as it smashed into my door
And I lay there in a crumpled heap - all battered, bruised and sore.
But at least my luck's now better, for as I saw its load give way,
I was buried thickly by manure - my garden should be great in May!

Paul Sanders

CANINE-MARES

Our dog had canine-mares, he had them every night
We think he dreamt of mouldy bones and cats that flew like kites.

Who'd dive-bomb him with doggy combs and bars of doggy-soap
The vet said he was terrified and gave him little hope.

He bit the vet who's not well yet and says he'll sue our dog
Which gives our poor maligned pet more reasons still to stop.

But now we've found an answer, at least we hope we have
We give him cheese and boiled peas to send him to the lav.

He's up all night and that's alright, he cannot dream at all
Problem is his breaking wind echoes round the hall.

And rising up the smell erupts and keeps us from repose
But sleep will come to a weary heart with a peg upon its nose.

Whilst table games and earplug wax ease the longest hours
New hobbies too like fungus growing - the air's not good for flowers.

Peter Asher

THE PATTERN OF TIE-IN EFFETE

For Pashmina's mother, high fashion is all
So she wears the name of Mamma's latest shawl.
The first-born, still boldest, says nothing shocks her
Since finding Great-Grandmother's precious fox fur
Had furnished the proud and unique name she'd bear:
There's no other Tippet of whom she's aware!
Now, some did suspect she was having a joke
On hearing that Daughter-Mark-Two was called Cloak
And anti-apartheid friends tended to gape
When told the third fruit of her loins would be Cape.
Her eldest boy altered his name by deed poll:
Gold Lamé was fine - but he never liked Stole.
When younger, her twin sons' behaviour was weird
Though wet blanket Poncho has since disappeared
While therapy treatment the other required
Persuaded Serape his name was inspired.
This child-bearing passion must now face a gap
Till fashion decrees there's a new style of wrap.
I have a vague notion we'll find likely clues
In 'Vogue' for the names future issue will use!

Andrew Buchanan

ODE FROM A CHAUVINIST

Be my love now and forever
I'm big and strong and very clever.

I'll make you happy every day
If you don't answer back and do as I say.

In time you'll see that I'm always right
So be my woman, don't put up a fight.

I'll exercise daily and flex my pecs
In return for some rampant sex.

Claire Bradford

THE HAT - FROM JAPAN

It's most definitely here to stay
at a jaunty angle, or any old way
in *powder-blue* - yes, that one will do!
He certainly must have been last in the queue.

He could have had a nice *Panama*
But with one or two hours spent in the bar,
his fashion sense had wandered afar
Well, this is what happens to a *'Jolly Jack Tar'*

Norm reckons he looks really *hip*
But he looks more like he's just *jumped ship*.
When Norm arrived at his front door,
his wife just couldn't believe what she saw.

'What's that on your head?' is all she said,
'Looks like it's been *pummelled* and left for dead.'
'Er, it's me new hat, it cost sixty yen.'
'Well that's just like you Norm
You've been seen off - *again*.'

Norman H McGlasham

OUR OLD HOUSE

We moved from our old house a few years ago
Since then the repairs on it have been very slow.
But now when I pass, I am happy to see,
That bricklaying, plastering and even carpentry
Are transforming the old place into something unknown,
That someone will welcome as a place called home.

Looking back, what makes me laugh
Is dragging in the old tin bath.
From its nail on the garden wall
We brought it in by the kitchen stool,
Then with saucepans and kettles of boiling water
We had our bath where we didn't oughter!
Now when I relax in my fibre-glass
I look back upon the past
Who else could bath and make the tea
And through a crack in the door watch TV!

Betty Glanville

FOOTBALL CRAZY

She stands at the altar
With a beautiful smile
If I could but tell her
She'd run a fast mile.

Has nobody warned her?
What she has to face
From a man who loves football
And boots with a lace.

Well now wedding's over
She's married her mate
They stand with the knife poised
Above a tiered cake.

But what is now happening
As guests start to cheer
'He's off to the match, love
And a Boddington's beer.'

Edith Pilkington

Forces Favourite

A Forces favourite was Madame La Gonga,
Who danced in shimmies and sometimes a tonga.
She was waltzing to things composed by Strauss
When the Polizei entered and shouted 'Raus!'

But the men of the law were not amused
(They were sometimes assaulted and always abused)
To have to cut short La Gonga's sky-larking:
They'd rather nab drivers for naughty parking.

La Gonga, however, would not be denied,
And danced till the eggs and bacon were fried.
She then gave the policemen a buckshee treat
By dancing in nowt but a pair of bare feet.

The Polizei did not make report
On a lady they thought who didn't ought
To dance around in nighties and slippers -
A mother, they knew, of ten little nippers.

So Gonga tripped on, kicking higher and higher,
Accompanied now by a male voice choir.
They sang, as she danced, with all their might,
Whether sober or sloshed or just a bit tight.

The show won no prizes or Emmy Awards,
And sometimes they fell right through the floorboards.
But the chorus maintained a stiff upper lip,
It was worth an earthquake to see Gonga strip.

A mother of ten she may well have been,
But when seen in the buff she stayed good and seen,
Old soldiers believed that life was worthwhile
When she beamed on them with her famous bare smile.

She danced for the padres as well as the troops -
Their anthems of praise were more like war whoops.
But she met her end one night in the nude,
And fell off the pier at RAF Bude.

K Cox

BENEATH THE WHISPER

Beneath the whisper within the glade
Under the trees in the dell
Along the banks of the riverside
Is where the fairies dwell.

They dwell in the shade of tree and bloom
And shelter there during the day
But when the sun goes down at night
It's then that the fairies play.

They play and dance and skip about
By the light of a moon-filled sky
They fly like birds upon the wing
Singing as they pass by.

As they pass those also here within
The butterflies, glow-worms and bees
They sing with delight to these friends of the night
While gaily chasing a breeze.

They chase a breeze then stop a while
To rest in this magical dell
Beneath the whisper within the glade
Where all the fairies dwell.

Jean Phillips

LIFE MUST GO ON

On a sad, wet day in March you were laid to rest
Tears mingled with rain, love put to the ultimate test.
My eyes hypnotised by the grave of our baby son
My mind drifted back to the day you carried his coffin,
                              his short life over and done.
It transported me back a million years,
Saying goodbye to life created by us; our combined tears.
Now you lay only a few feet away from that little boy
Which is as it should be for the births of our children
                              brought us such joy.
Yet, I would recoil from reliving again the pain on our
                              children's faces when you went away,
Sorrow, regret, nostalgia, such mixed emotions on that sad, sad day.
The black abyss I inhabit I have to break free of, for this is life,
Life must go on, no matter how hard, so full of pain and full of strife.
Procreation has taken place and from our love two infants are
                              about to be born
Two new grandchildren about to greet the world with their
                              first new-born yawn.

M A Shipp Yule

MEGAN'S FIRST COMMUNION

Today we watched Megan all dressed in white
It was indeed a most beautiful sight
Megan was making her First Communion
Today with God she made her union.

The look on the children's faces this morning
Showed us for them a new era was dawning
We pray Dear God their lives be long
May their minds be healthy and their will be strong.

We all love Megan she belongs to our clan
And we try to be true and good as we can
We were all so proud of her today
For her, a long happy life, we Pray.

Jill Dryden

WEEKEND BREAK

We cruised around for hours
Sea mist descending fast
After seeking out directions
We find the road at last.

I'm sure it's past this chippy
No, no, it's down this lane,
We drive around the corner,
To come right back again.

On at last, arriving, we are
Greeted at the door expectations
Of warm welcome, quickly dashed
Upon the floor.

Gong is sounding now for dinner
Hurry up we want to taste,
Banks on order from the forecourt
Hurry in, no time to waste.

Thoughts of food upon the table
Made our flagging spirits soar
All eyes turn without exception
Eagerly to face the door.

Plates arrive, all hot before us,
Would have been so grand but I'm a
Vegetarian and there were eggs and ham.

Patricia Mullins

RAGGEDY RHUBARB

Raggedy rhubarb leaves
Flapping foliage everywhere
Slippery snails on green, with
Gaping gashes here and there

Steeped and steaming slices
Bleeding, not a beetroot in sight
Raucous reds and gangrenous greens
Tasty tantalising delight

Sweet sugars for this here stew
Naughty nutmeg to flavour the brew
Hocus-pocus cast aside
Dig deep little spoon and enjoy the ride.

Thomas J Baker

YOU'RE THE CAT'S WHISKERS

My girlfriend had just left me
So I was feeling sad and lonely
When suddenly you flitted into the room
Like a model on the catwalk
But I could see you were no phoney
And the left side of my chest just went boom.

There was no pause or hesitation
You looked so lovely in your fur coat
Move into my flat this afternoon
Leave that man in Berkeley Mews
With his mistress up in Eastcote
Stay with me or life will be a mournful tune.

I've heard those dreadful rumours
Of your nights out on the tiles
How you're affected by the phases of the moon
But it's only half expected
With those charming feminine wiles
Promise Tiddles that you'll come and live here soon.

Stuart Delvin

VIETNAM POEM

Here you look behind your back
Rifle ready to bark
For eyes that burn like an AK round
That always finds its mark
Bourbon slips down Tennessee throats
Easily slit in the dark
F4s thunder
Whores know where
They heard some careless remark
And GI's return
In body bags
Stacked
By an armoured vehicle park.

Paul Wilkins

TABLE

I sat on my own
All alone
At a table
With Clarke Gable
Drinking wine
Feeling fine
I punched a bloke
Dealing Coke
I nicked his stuff
And had a puff
Feeling fine
Drinking wine
With Clarke Gable
At a table
I'm all alone
On my own.

Helen Minazza-Sturt

EULOGY FOR DIANA

To you the future king was born
No happier day could ever dawn
Thus did your royal role start
Later played, alas with breaking heart.

Posthumous words tried to assuage
The misery of palace days,
We pray the dreadful price you paid
Will show the need for kindlier ways.

Your beauty bewitched us all
When all alone at the Taj Mahal.
Your will no protocol could bend
You treated all as dearest friend.

Your life, unsuited to Scotland's glen's,
Often pursued by camera's lens,
Still lives for us, as well it might,
Bravely you fought for what was right.

Let this epitaph be thine
'You did your best for all mankind
Rest in peace, do not repine
They have banned the dreadful mine.'

G Nicklin

SUMMERTIME BLUES

It's been a typical English summer
With the beat of the falling rain.
It made Wimbledon fortnight a washout,
And the cricket is called off - again!

On our beaches the deckchairs are dripping,
And the kids are all growing webbed feet.
The neighbours have gone to Majorca
To escape all the gales and the sleet.

We should have been getting a suntan
While lazing about on the sand.
But our bikinis are still in the suitcase
And nothing is going as planned.

We've dreamed all the year of this fortnight,
Just two weeks of bliss in the sun.
Was that too much to ask for, we wonder,
Being soaked through each day is no fun.

But are we downhearted, we Britons?
As our holiday's ruined once more.
No. We've still got our great sense of humour,
To shine through the wettest downpour.

E Crowhurst

WINTERS OF YESTERDAY

Misty mornings, early warnings
Winter's here, to stay
Late November, do you remember
Winters of yesterday.

Times when the snow, pure and white
Fell in flurries on bright starry nights.

Building snowmen, coal for eyes
Looking upwards, icy skies.

Frozen ponds on which to skate
So impatient, we couldn't wait.

Snowy hills, down we sped
Fingers freezing, nose bright red.

Snowball fights, we never lost
Remember seeing, old Jack Frost.

Yes I remember winter's gone
How it's changed as years roll on.

Now we only stand and gaze
Wishing away these cold bleak days.

The snow now not quite so white
The stars don't shine quite so bright.

Times passed by and along the way
We lost the winters of yesterday.

Sharon Salt

AND LET THE WORLD KEEP TURNING

She came from the Antipodes
And didn't like our winter trees,
They look so cold, she said.

I didn't like her evergreen
And gloomy 'bush' - no changing scene
Of seasons going by.

Her Christmas was a sunny meal,
For me it had a phoney feel
Under its cloudless sky.

If East is East and West is West,
To each the land where he can rest
And let the world keep turning.

For North and South this will not do,
We're up to us and down to you,
We call it a Divide.

Don't cross it with a baggage
Of Saints and Holidays,
Abandon all and start again -
Adopt the local ways.
Or, stay at home and never roam
And let the world keep turning.

Clare Meadmore

DON'T

Don't put me in that kind of cage,
where you must stay in constant rage
and life has to fit on a special page,
that office with its suit of beige
and Sunday dinners with some sage,
those weekly friends who dance upon a stage,
until their arteries commence blockage,
they feed themselves the same message,
comply with us you've reached that certain age,
I have no wish to disparage,
but, individuals could meet with damage
and find themselves the subject of carnage.

Jean Paisley

THE MEETING

Aimless heart, empty eyes, terminal fate realised,
She stands and barely sips warm drink,
Crying cold stare at the rain, bare flaked window frame,
Drab robe turns back on cracked white sink.

Young elbows cradled tight, the onslaught of night,
She supports the agony of invisible pain,
Lifeless room gives way, to neon street at play
Dulls faded wallpaper, with ancient stain.

One movement of warm head, she delays thoughts of bed,
Memory dulls the past days of fun,
She spies leaning your man, boasting rain lacquered tan,
It's clear, he's waiting loved one.

Rain droplets like pearls, her body uncurls,
Her blue eyes become transfixed,
Biting lip, expectant sigh, she darts passers by,
Her emotional cocktail mixed.

Another hopeful, no, yes, again a guess,
Young man turns up collar to cold,
Which mystery friend, this waiting to end?
Shudders at her thoughts so increasingly bold.

Reckless moment so rare, she tidies her hair,
She's going down the street!
Heart beating tattoo, she trips over shoe,
Leaves behind draft window seat.

Breathless coat up tight, she enters the night,
Rain cold, and sooty black ink,
Young man no longer there, half smile, fusses hair,
And looks up at the room with the cracked white sink.

Robert G Goodman

THE FIRE OF LOVE

Sometimes when you ignite a fire,
It may flare quickly like desire,
Or when kindling makes a tiny spark,
Love gropes blindly in the dark.

As the heat increases, lovers dance,
To the roar of true romance,
Flaming tongues spiral, leaping higher,
Hearts are melting as they aspire.

To reach the height
Of true delight,
Bask in the glow
That lovers know,
Blistering yearning,
Passions burning,
Depth of feeling,
Sends them reeling.
The flame of love,
Soaring above
Mere mortal plane,
Returned again,
Searing ended,
Souls are blended
In warmth and peace,
Never to cease.

Unless the incandescence ceases,
Love extinguished to minute pieces,
But if a flicker struggles on,
Fan it hard or love is gone.

Helen Mitchelhill

Always

Mother so sweet
you've always been there.
To wipe away tears
and to show that you care.

I will love you forever
but no words, you see,
Could tell you exactly
what you mean to me.

Marion McGarrigle

Rain

Splish; splash.
Watching the rain.
The smoothest of rivulets
On the roughest terrain.

Splash; splish.
Catching the drips.
The circles of water
Soften all that they hit.

Crash; bang.
A thunder-filled sky.
Flashes of lightning
And a grumbling sigh.

Bang; crash.
Wet spots on the path.
The break of the clouds
Or a sign of God's wrath?

Suie Nettle

TROUBLES TO PEARLS

The oyster lay on the deep sea bed,
Suddenly in trouble.
A speck of sand entered his shell,
And he was seeing double.

Poor oyster felt the pain so much,
But couldn't push it out.
It pricked and prodded him inside
And he began to shout.

'I can't go on like this!' he cried,
Becoming yet more sore.
He fought against this agony.
It beat him all the more.

Then all at once he had a plan
To deal with all the grit.
And after enduring a very long time
It didn't hurt a bit.

Instead of all the ugliness
That caused his irritation,
A lovely pearl was formed around
This awful tribulation.

I'd like to learn a lesson
From things I tend to foister,
To turn my troubles into pearls
Just like that wise old oyster.

Judith Thomas

ANOTHER PLACE - SCAMP'S

After brave, blind Tara died,
She left an aching void inside.
Another golden bitch might fill
The vacant place and anguish still?

At the time that's how it felt,
But fate, another card had dealt.
Confusion reigned; I didn't know
Which bitch to have, or where to go!

For every time I almost had one,
I drew back, so there was none.
At last I knew I couldn't face
A golden bitch in Tara's place.

And so it was with love and joy
There came a jet black Cocker boy.
And even before he came in sight,
Intuition told me he was right.

And though dear Tara mourn I still,
And though her place Scamp doesn't fill,
His coming marks another phase,
Another dog - Another place.

Ina Harrington

HIS FIRST JOB

Our high garden hedge is eight foot three
With Christmas coming he would not see
Our distant view of downs and hills
So grandson Christopher brought his saw
And cut it down to five foot four,
At the end of the day, we saw Monét thrills
Highdown hills and Cissbury Ring
Then we heard our school children sing

'Christmas time
Whatever the weather
Always to rhyme
Love and peace forever.'
Amen.

Paff-Pafford

TWENTY-TWO LINES

Thou' art the word that never ends
Thou' art the height where man ascends
Thou' art the ruler of justice and law,
Thou' art the hand and the straw
Thou' art the theme of life it's retainer
Thou' art the strength the power of sustainer
Thou' art the voice of truth to hear
Thou' art the light from darkness and fear
Thou' art the back that never breaks
Thou' art the hand that never takes
Thou' art the heartbeat the sanctum the glory
Thou' art the beginning and the end of life's story
Thou' art the thought of every man's mind
Thou' art the sands that limit the time
Thou' art the sea that surrounds every shore
Thou' art the Zenith where there is no more
Thou' art the throne that rules alone
Thou' art the supreme spirit, not the flesh and bone
The royal King the Sovereign the spherical sphere
'Espirit De Corps' where thou' goest there go I, I am there I am here,
Who 'art' thee that question! . . . I . . . am!
The all knowing - the heart - the soul - of the man.

A B Lawson

OUT OF TOWN

Away from the noise and the squalor
Litter and shattered glass
To the sweetly winding river
And banks of emerald grass
Sweet-smelling breezes of summer
Echoing through the trees
And instead of the throb of engines
The busy murmur of bees.

A meadow sprinkled with flowers
Reflecting the stars at night
Birdsong instead of transistors
Swelling the hours of light.
May the countryside of England
Help make the spirit whole
And the God-given gifts of Nature
Be a balm to injured souls.

The rippling waves of the lake-shore
The buoyant clouds on high
The music of winds through the treetops
Low breezes that gently sigh
The lapping waters calling
Tempting the sunbeams to play
And break and mend in the flowing
And dance in the feathered spray.

Iris Reeves

KISSED BY A STAR

She was only a child and she could not sleep
She closed her eyes and then she would peep,
Out of the window to the sky of blue
Where early flowers were wet with dew.
Her curly head on the pillow lay
But she could not sleep, it was a special day,
Daddy was returning from his voyage to sea
Home at last - she giggled with glee.
She had gazed at the stars and with earnest prayer
Begged them to twinkle and guide him everywhere.
Now Daddy would be home from his travels afar
To be with his child, who was kissed by a star.

Jean Mackenzie

STATE OF BEING

These days I sit and dream and watch the world go by,
I see the seasons pass beneath a changing sky,
The restless, drifting clouds, the sunshine and the rain,
The falling of the leaves and wind against the pane.

I wonder at the stars, and at the sunset's glow,
The music of a stream, and fields covered in snow.
Behind a veil of ferns I can pretend to be
A raindrop or a bird, or waves upon the sea.

Beyond the open door today the world is still;
Somewhere in the distance a tractor climbs a hill.
Sunlight dappled foliage on gently swaying trees,
Sunkissed golden grasses are rippling in the breeze.

Through the kaleidoscope of my own private world,
An ever shifting scene as each day is unfurled.
Endless is the cycle and lovely is the song,
Timeless are the cosmos to which we all belong.

I wish I could bequeath my love of simple things,
My oneness with nature and all the peace it brings.
I have become the 'now' of what was yesterday;
Banished are the shadows and clearer is the way.

Rosina Winiarski

Sing Unto The Lord

Sing unto the Lord, sing unto his name,
Sing unto the Lord, from heaven to earth he came.
So sing a song of victory,
Of peace and joy and love,
That he who came to earth to die
Now lives in heaven above.

Sing unto the Lord, sing unto his name.
Sing unto the Lord, to Bethlehem he came.
Of Virgin born, in manger laid,
By angel choir adored,
The Shepherds saw a Saviour
Who is Jesus Christ the Lord.

Sing unto the Lord, sing unto his name,
Sing unto the Lord, to Galilee he came.
The lame did walk, the dead were raised,
The blind received their sight.
He said I am the Way, the Truth,
The Life, the Bread, the Light.

Sing unto the Lord, sing unto his name,
Sing unto the Lord, to Calvary he came.
So sing a song of suffering,
Of anguish and of pain,
To save our souls from Satan's power,
He died and rose again.

Sing unto the Lord, sing unto his name,
Sing unto the Lord, to Olivetr he came.
His work complete, the victory won,
To heaven he went again,
Head of his Church, to wait the day,
When he returns to reign.

A E Turner

THE WAYWARD WIND

I am a frolicsome, wayward wind,
Blowing this way and that,
Whisking away that girl's silk scarf,
Or maybe - that gent's hat.

I am a soft and gentle breeze,
Wafting on warm summer days.
Ruffling a careful hairdo, or
Cooling the sun's hot rays.

I am a mean and angry gale,
Throwing my weight about.
What do I care? Oer hills and dale,
The damage I do? There's no doubt!

I am a scary, stormy wind,
Tossing things in my way -
Fences and gates share the same fate!
I am king of all I survey!

I am a raging, violent typhoon,
Screaming my own special song,
Moving at speed: Taking no heed,
Enjoying my strength as I hurtle along.

Today, (in a fog) I'm just drifting about,
Too tired to bother, and can't find my way,
(But I've had my moments, loud screams and shouts,)
So I'll take it easy - till another day!

Ivy Cawood

LEFTOVER

What happened lover
To my life in clover
When did my selfless service become redundant?
Cease to be a treasured, guarantee covenant
Nothingness, discarded, disregarded waste
Yesterday, the day before bad taste
You are sure; you can do without -
Without me, the love in your heart, cast out

Treating me as rubbish
What does he hope to accomplish
Once his appetiser, once his desire, hot coals, not ash
In the window of his soul, now, I appear as trash
Endlessly I satisfied his needs, couldn't see, he was vain
Tirelessly he drank in my sweetness; more was
                        his lover's only complain
Roaring wide, wild, his puppy dog face lit-up like
                        next door's Rover
At last, fee from him, I have love to share, a heat-wave
                        that'll never blow over.

Rosetta Stone

OUR DOGS

Our dogs to us are a sheer delight
We saw them and knew that they were right
To rescue them was our intent
And knew they're coming to us was meant
One is brown and well laid back
To be loved by all that is his knack
The other one is black and tan
In a fight he'd be your man
Together they're a perfect pair
They've taken over every chair
Our lives are richer, busier now
How we managed before we know not how
Their daily walk it is a must
In every way we have their trust
So when in doubt, rescue a pet
This we know you'll not regret
You'll find you have a lot less stress
For they will bring just happiness.

Norah Bennett

FLORIDA'S NATURE COAST

Fish jump high in the Crystal River.
Pampas grass stand stately and tall.
Ferns sway in the morning breeze,
The rising sun crowns it all.

Endangered Manatees glide in the Mexican Gulf,
Natural warm springs surround Kings Bay.
Cruise boats anchor near the pier
A school of dolphins enjoy their play.

Impatient boats stand in secure moorings,
The boardwalk stretches long and wide,
Coloured butterflies flutter through the reed grass,
Nature and beauty sit side by side.

Elizabeth Hunter

THE HOUSE

I used to think I owned this house,
But now I sometimes wonder,
The sparrow on the roof, and under
The pile of logs, the mouse
Regard this as their own domain.
No thought of maintenance or rates,
Repairing fences, mending gates,
Enters their little brain,
The cats, regarding it as theirs,
Return each day to slumber
And rodents without number
Fall victim to their snares,
While my old dog patrols the bounds -
(She knows the house is hers)
And, by her vigilance deters
Marauding, alien hounds,
Even the spider in the hall
Considers this her home,
The very earthworm in the loam,
The fly upon the wall,
So many worlds revolve around
This ancient pile of stone,
But, by my single self alone,
Its upkeep must be found!

Dorothy Steadman

THE LITTLE FOX

A fox was playing in the woods one day,
when there came a familiar sound.
She knew at once she must get away,
as pattering paws she heard on the ground.
The little fox knew that the hunt had begun,
'Oh why must they chase me?' - she cried.
In terror she continued to run,
looking for somewhere to hide.
The terrified fox sped round the trees,
then felt she could run no more.
She cried out to God through the whispering breeze;
'Please help me it's You I adore,'
God heard the prayer of His little child,
and then in His mercy and love.
A divine angel so gentle and mild,
He sent down from Heaven above.
The little fox saw a beautiful light,
and then gave a gentle sigh.
For she was held in loving arms so tight,
and with joy she began to cry.
The angel said; 'Don't cry, but be glad
that the Father loves both great and small.
And we in Heaven are all very sad,
when we listen to the huntsman's call.
One day this world will be as Heaven above,
when all wars and cruelty will cease.
The earth will abound with God's divine love,
and then everyone will find His peace.
The angel took the little fox home,
her family were full of delight.

Never again did the little fox roam,
she was protected by the angel of light.
Many years later the fox gave a sigh,
her eyes she shut gently to sleep.
Then the angel returned and lifting her high,
took God's child into Heaven to keep.

Nicky Young

ON THE BEACH

Hands in pockets, three men stood
By the Archimedes Screw,
Washed up by the tide's full flood,
Thinking *Just what can we do*
With this Archimedes Screw,
Sixty feet long and twelve feet wide,
Laid like a sleeping spiral slide!
Thirty tons, at least, it will weigh.
However could it go astray?

      'Is it lost? What does it do?'

'Stood up, turning round and round,
(Sorry! I assumed you knew!)
It lifts grain up from the ground,
Also water, up and round
Once a wellspring has been found.'

      'It's very cold and wet out here.
      Photo-call's over. We can go.
      A bowl of soup is my idea.
      You can check up on what you know.'

    'We'd best find an encyclopaedia,
    And brush up on our Archimedia!'

Louie Carr

WHITE HORSE OF ANDALUSIA

White horse of Andalusia
through sugar lump Granada go.
On saddle of Nevada snow
bear bold Apocalypse.
Dream clouds in dumb adagio
begowned in down and candleglow -
tame White Dove of El Rocio
besieged by fingertips.

White horse of Andalusia
competing with horizon flash
of shattered thunderbolts you thrash
amazed mankind aloof.
Your leaping heart, your whetted brain,
cascading tail, wind-bannered mane
electrify wide ochre plane
that shrivels under hoof.

White horse of Andalusia
cavorting in the zodiac
Iago commandeers your back
to rout the infidel.
You hurdle monumental seas.
Incredulous the Indian flees
abandoning divinities.
A flying caravel!

White horse of Andalusia
wade deep your skies of lavender.
Soon elegant rejoneador
constructs his cruel pyre.
Black tortured bull. Volcanic scorn.
Descendant of the unicorn
transfixed upon a lethal horn
dissolve in crimson fire.

Peter Gillott

Christmas Eve

It's Christmas eve, there's lots to do,
There's puddings to make and mince pies too.
There's presents to wrap with shiny string,
While at our door the carollers sing.
We're feeling tired, we rub our eyes,
We hang our stockings for our surprise.
St Nicholas is on his way,
Bells are ringing on his sleigh.
He rides along through starry skies,
With a jolly laugh and twinkling eyes.
The children snuggle down in bed,
With dreams of Santa in their heads.

Jane Carter

BRAMLEY COURT

I'm in sheltered housing at Bramley Court,
It really is just fine.
There's roses on archways and lavender walks,
All bright and scented in the lovely sunshine.

Cynthia our warden is a jolly lady
And we await her morning call -
Asking 'Are you alright love?'
And we assure her that the night was not bad at all.

There's coffee mornings and bingo
And some of us play Scrabble
And the coach trip to the seaside
We might be brave and paddle.

Some of us have walking frames
And others have walking sticks,
Whilst some must have a wheelchair
And be pushed around for ???

Oh! There'll be lots of fun and things to do
And quite a lot of chatter
And who said, 'If they have fish and chips,
They'll not be eating batter!'

I'll probably ride the train to Pakefield
And sit in the gardens there
And then ride back to town
And have a cup of tea on the pier.

And to end up the day,
I'll choose a treat
And buy the biggest ice cream
All chocolate and nutty and sweet.

Maureen Williams

THE KISS

I walked along
The sun was warming
I hadn't got a care
This lovely morning
When suddenly I spied a friend
Oh no I thought
This is the end
She threw her arms round
Gave me a kiss
She left a mark
That you couldn't miss
I sorted for tissues in my pocket
Not there oh dear
I must have forgot it
So hand to cheek
I covered the bow
Made excuses to all
To the dentist to go
Sympathy saved me
Till I reached home
My folks were out
I was quite alone
I looked in the mirror
I knew I would see
A great scarlet bow
As red as could be
The soap and the water
Were not very kind
My rubbing and scrubbing
Left a red patch behind.

Betty Puddefoot

MERRY DANCE

Music I have
A taste for it all
When I was younger
There was many a ball
To jive and to twist
To rock and to roll
I danced them all
As I recall
When the music starts
Playing the beat
The rhythm takes over
I'm tapping my feet
On and on thru me it flows
From the top of my head
Right down to my toes
I'm at one with the tune
To the end I will croon
It makes me feel great
Fred Astaire has a mate
As soon as the music
Starts to play
I'm off again
Jigging away!

Fritzi Newlands-Du'Barry

WELLHOUSE COTTAGE

An idyllic cottage with a glorious view,
Two centuries old and nothing new
Surrounded by farmland, oh yes it's all true,
But . . .
Why wasn't I told of the holes in the roof,
Of water that drips to the floor
Why wasn't I told of the sewer that leaks,
Into the farmland right next to my door,
Of the mice that coming visiting every night,
I know by their bits on the floor.
Why wasn't I told of the yearly events,
That farmers do every day,
The ploughing of land, the raising of crops,
The tractors, the seagulls, clouds of hay?
But greater by far, the spreading of muck
It brings you good fortune they say.
I only know the smell is so bad
I stay in closed windows all day.
No gardening for me, it really is grim
Invading my life in that way,
But wait, see the view, the sun has appeared,
My doubts are now all blown away.

Josephine Grinham

LAST LOVE

It's very quiet now
Since last you slammed the door and went away.
I never came to understand quite how
The differences we had could set in play
Such noise, or even more
That slamming door.

Is this the last time then
That you will threaten to abandon me
Upon a whim, upon a toss, or when
The stress of life means finally
That homeward roads are jammed
And my door slammed.

It should be quiet still;
Oh but the thrashing of unease is here.
And what can quiet offer to fulfil
Sound of a voice, a welcome, though I fear
Peace will not come again
Bereft of pain.

Joan Gordon

LIFE'S MAZE

I don't need
Any recognition.
I can live without praise,
But,
I need
A little kindness,
To help me,
Through
Life's Maze.

Christa Todd

WINTER TREES

In the quiet of my day
I watch the trees in gentle sway.
Bare branched arms reach out to me
They wave and beckon, come be free.
The wind is kind to them today,
Soft breath upon those branches grey.
See the frail sparrows jostle in the breeze.
Seeking comfort and shelter amongst the wintry trees.
Soon the snow will fall, a canopy of cold white
Will drape the trees, hiding the knots and knarls from sight.
In grandeur they stand, they still call to me.
Perceive their evergreen souls beneath that dignity.

Jean Wharldall

A Villanelle To Dawn

Sweet song of birds proclaims the death of night,
Weak rays of sun herald the dawn of day.
The whole world stirs in turn with growing light.

The dull red orb is changed to gleaming bright,
God-fearing people kneel at their beds to pray,
Sweet song of birds proclaims the death of night.

The blindness caused by dark is changed to sight
And children's fears the shining beams allay.
The whole world stirs in turn with growing light.

To wake sound sleepers shrill alarms incite
While weary workers plod with clods of clay.
Sweet song of birds proclaims the death of night.

All forms of life thrive in warmth of sun's might,
Sent down to earth with every blinding ray.
The whole world stirs in turn with growing light.

So day by day black darkness is vanquished quite,
Revolving earth within its path will stay.
Sweet song of birds proclaim the death of night.
The whole world stirs in turn with growing light.

Hywel Davies

WHY POETRY IS SUCH FUN?

Poetry means the world to me,
It's better than netball or watching TV.
I read 'em in the morning,
Read 'em at night,
Read 'em in black, purple or white,
Poems about giraffes, crocodiles and pigs,
Poems about men in funny orange wigs,
Poems that are hot,
Poems that are cold,
Poems in italics,
Poems in bold.
So come on people take a look,
It's always fun to read a poetry book!

O A Daley

THE FISHER'S OF LONDON

They ask me to do a rhyme
About the fisher life of older time
So I put some fine words down
How they lived in London town.
Augustine he wed Rebecca there
And met the family of one John Clare.
Soon a story I could tell
About Elizabeth Clare from Clerkswell
To Holborn the tram did take her
Where she met William - a mantle maker.

Soon they had children one by one
There in St Lukes in eighteen fifty-one,
Another branch of the fisher tree
That help to bring the birth to me
In that day before the car
The family did not travel far
In nineteen hundred, the family did go
To my old house in Walthamstow.
Now I have moved to old Leyton
And all the fisher line is gone.

Colin Allsop

RHYME ON

Good old fashioned rhyme, in all it's simplicity,
can sometimes be compiled, altruistically.
Or just for fun, to pass the quiet times away,
in diary form, in remembrance of an eventful day.
A simple inventive limerick, to amuse bored kids,
stop them from dissecting, another frogs eyelids!
It can be dedicated to the memory, of lost loved ones,
or celebrate the burning lust, of love's young guns.
Calm unsleepy children, hyperactive and awake,
used as a recipe instruction, to bake a perfect cake.
Be passed through the air, one silicon chip to another,
record fond memories, of a happy, well loved mother.
Make comment on world events, local goings on too,
wars seen all too often, baby panda born at the zoo.
Inspire hope, in a person feeling depressed and down,
cheering them up, like a daft smiling, rosy faced clown.
If you can use it, do so, for the time is right to rhyme on,
it could be the bandwagon you've been waiting for,
so why not take the chance, get rhyming, and climb on!

Danny Coleman

MOMENT OF TRUTH

The wheels of time keep turning,
   We can't put time on hold,
We've just to keep on learning
   As the leaves of time unfold . . .

Sometimes we would like to call a halt,
   And perhaps, just stop the clock,
Especially when life is rosy
   But, then things run amock . . .

And, as we reach maturity
   It's good to then look back,
It's then we start to realise
   How much we've gone off track . . .

Today's world is like a roller coaster,
   Moving at a terrific pace,
There is no time to stand and stare
   It's quite a different place . . .

From the world we knew in years gone by
   When life was so serene,
Oh, there were wars and poverty,
   But, a good life in between . . .

Then, I guess we got our priorities right,
   And money was never our God,
We attended church and Sunday school
   And were ruled with a golden rod . . .

Today, children are taught so differently
   And are given too much rope,
Discipline has gone out of the window
   And folks don't know how to cope . . .

Eileen Greenwood Sadler

WE LOVE YOU MANDY

Mandy you are everything to us all,
We love you very much, we would never be cruel.
You have given us years of love and companionship,
Sometimes though you're in my way and I suddenly trip.
You know every word we all say,
We can't bear to think we will loose you one day.
You get so excited when we come into the house,
Even though we try to be as quiet as a mouse.
You're a bit mad that is for sure,
We really try to come quietly through that door.
You don't stop jumping at us and it gets a bit frustrating,
But it really doesn't matter as into our hearts lots of love you bring.
The day we brought you home ten years ago you were
                                              small and cuddly,
You were to grow into a lovely dog that was plain to see,
A lovely poodle is what you are
And when we first saw you we fell in love with you from afar.

Karen Grover

IMPRESSIONS

Absent without leave from school,
The 'Incorrigible V;
Appeared from nowhere to inflict,
Her terrorism on me.
She had recently lost her mother,
And maybe was insecure;
Was that why she wanted someone to pay?
Well! I wasn't really sure.
So I gave her my school milk money,
Just to let me get away.

But arriving at school I was too late,
They had cleared the yard and closed the gate.

Then I saw the headmaster and tried to explain,
But he put me in line with the rest;
All my pleas were made in vain,
I would get three of the best,
While he practised his swing I stood there and froze,
And trembled at his invitation;
Then towering above me he stood on his toes,
My hands out in supplication,
Down came the cane and I felt such pain,
I almost died of fear:
It shot from my hand through my arm,
And forced me to bite back a tear.

Bullies are bullies whatever their form,
Does life make them that way or is that how they're born?

Then on to the grammar school and kind Mr B,
He didn't use the cane but made an impression on me.

June Lane

THE PINK TOOTHBRUSH

The pink toothbrush left home today,
So young and proud on her chosen way,
Acting perhaps just a little too gay,
Trying, no doubt, my fears to allay.

The taxi man gave me a comforting smile
As I helped him load boxes and sacks in a pile.
'I'm not going far, mam, just a couple of miles.'
As the taxi moved off, I stood for a while.

Today's like any other - so I thought -
Dogs to walk - food to be bought,
A call to make, a bus to be caught,
Forget all my dreams that had come to nought.

It was after tea before I dared
Enter the room which she had shared
With records and posters - no wall was spared -
It was then that I knew how much I cared.

You see, it was tidy - it just didn't look right,
No clutter of make-up, no discarded tights,
No clothes on the floor from the previous night.
I turned away quickly and switched off the light.

I was coping quite well, of that I was sure.
No need to worry - time was the cure -
A nice hot bath might help me procure
Relief from the pain, hope for the future.

The bath looked inviting - I sighed and lay back
I was really quite lucky - what did I lack?
Then the tears fell in torrents - there was no holding back
When I saw - no pink toothbrush there in the rack!

G E Tate

BLUE EYES

He's not tall and dark
He's short and grey
Yet he has stolen
My heart away.

His eyes are not brown
But all shapes of blue
Like ice when he's angry
And glaring at you.

I've heard in a song
What blue eyes can do
And I'm here to say
It's perfectly true.

Jacqueline Taylor

MUSE BLUES

What's up? I write in rhyme.
This shouldn't be a problem,
I do this all the time,
Drowsing off at night,
And bang, an idea's dawning
So, on will go the light.
It can't wait until morning.
You see, I just have to write,
Yet, here I sit, paper blank.
Can't think what can be wrong,
But, well, to be quite frank,
My get up and go, has finally gone.
For heavens sake, woe is me.
Alas, goodbye to fame,
A poet I shall never be
Old age has quenched the flame
But wait, just hold it there!
I think I feel a stirring,
The muse begins to call,
My cogs have started whirring.
Guess I'll send this after all.
It could be the last time
But hey, why am I worrying,
I'll always find a rhyme?

Brenda Söhngen

THE REAL FAIRY TALE

From afar a poor boy came,
He did not know this story,
He travelled just to seek his fame,
To find his own true glory.

He tried to act, he did his best,
But he couldn't act, so failed the test.
'Go back to school,' the stage boss said,
'Learn to write, try that instead.'

'You're good with words,' the stage boss said,
'I'll sponsor you through school.'
'I must succeed,' the young boy said,
'And show that I'm no fool.'

So off to school the young boy went,
The stage boss kindly paid his rent.
He learnt his words and he became
A scholar who would achieve great fame.

Within six years he'd written a book,
Then that same year, another.
He wrote of things of which he knew
In fairy tales and others.

Soon he knew his fame had spread,
His success it had been proved,
The fame he'd sought had his become,
His tales today still read.

So let's give thanks to the old stage boss
Who treated the boy as his son.
Without his help we would have surely lost
Hans Christian Anderson.

Brenda Jane Williams

HAPPY DAYS

Write a poem about myself, what is there to say?
I don't know anyone famous, and each one's, just an ordinary day.
If I think back to my childhood, and really tax my brain,
I can still remember, how frightened I was, to have my
                                              first ride on a train.
Happy family holidays, good times, with Dad, and Mum,
Playing happily with simple toys, lost in the innocence of fun.
Then the pain of teenage years brought spots, and greasy hair,
Mini skirts, flares and medallions, were fashions beyond compare.
Hair piled up like beehives, eye make up black as pitch,
No wonder Father made comments, about falling in a ditch!
At seventeen I'm worldly wise, no doubt, I'm Belle of the Ball,
At home I've been re-christened - I'm now known as, 'Know All.'
How many times in those days did I miss the last bus home?
I couldn't help it that we weren't on the phone.
And then I'd meet my poor old Dad, coming up the street,
Despatched my Mum, to look for me, his slippers still on his feet.
'Why don't you think of others?' he would always calmly say,
'You know when we get home to Mother, there'll be hell to pay.'
And though I always threatened to go and rent a flat,
I really was quite relieved, when they took no notice of that.
So as I sit back to write this, it seems like yesterday,
It's hard to believe these memories are thirty years away.
Maybe once I did believe each one's just an ordinary day,
But each one brings a memory, to cherish, in a very special way.

L Liggett

ANGEL

With wings of feather and hair so fair,
An angel to teach us to love and care.
With his eyes of blue,
We would see reflections lord of you.
With his cloth of brilliant white,
There to guide us through the darkest night.
With his gentle hands that are unfurled,
To lead us through this mad, mad world.
With sandled feet that have walked before,
This my angel in my dream I saw.

A P Starling

MY DAD

The person I admire the most
That's you my loving dad
You're always there to comfort me
When I'm sick or sad.

You're always there to guide me
And you taught me wrong to right
That's why I want to tell you dad
You are my guiding light.

And when I was just little
With all my scares and fears
You were always there to cuddle me
And wipe away my tears.

But now that I have grown up
And sometimes my mind's a twirl
The one thing I will always be
That's my daddy's little girl.

So thanks for always being there
Through the good times and the bad
And to say how much I love you
For I'm so proud that you're my dad.

Isobel Campbell

Rain

Where does it really come from?
Do we really know?
Has it got a house up there?
Does it stay with snow?

Why does it fall at angles?
Is it that way inclined?
Read up books of knowledge
Few answers you will find!

Where does it really come from?
From clouds, it may perhaps
But that seems hardly likely,
We know it comes from taps!

So when it rains just bear in mind,
The rain that falls is wet,
It makes us cold and miserable,
An umbrella we can't forget!

So when it rains, just think about,
The mysteries unexplained,
We all had less on our minds,
Until the day it rained!

Andrew Dickson

MY DREAM BOY

Boys and girls go out to play,
I wish the boy over there would stay,
Come over here and ask me out,
Then invite me into his house.

Where there we would talk
And have a quick kiss
But things like that,
I can only wish.

Cause nothing like that will happen to me,
That boy's gone in for tea!

On the other hand, some boys are brats,
They stink and smell, just like rats.

But the boy I am describing,
Is nothing like that,
He is kind and caring,
As cute as a cat.

I am waiting here,
Just to see,
If my dream boy,
Will come to me.

Louise Collins

THE DENIM ANGEL

A flick of her hair as she walks past the crowd.
Cheers screaming and echoing loud.
Her paint-stained dungarees and DM's below,
Her greasy hair nurtured just to show
That angels don't need halos to make them pure.
It all boils down to something more.
Don't despise her as she takes her crown
Applaud, because the denim angel is in town.

Charlotte Lythgoe

MUMMY'S DAY OUT

Mummy Mouse had finished her chores,
Made the beds and swept the floors,
Made a cheese pie for dinner that night,
Then looked at the clock and squeaked with delight.
The day was still early, and now she was free,
'I'll go to the beach,' she laughed, happily.

Daddy was working so he'd never know,
Children at school, so they couldn't go,
She felt a bit naughty, but it would be good fun
To go off for the day without anyone.
She took off her apron and tidied her hair,
It wouldn't take long on her bike to get there.

Mummy Mouse ran her feet through the sand,
And looked at the shells she held in her hand,
How pretty they looked, so lovely to see,
'I'll look for some more to take home with me.
The children will love them - but then they would know
That I have been here, when they couldn't go.'

Her eyes lit up, she'd had an idea,
'At the weekend, I'll bring them both here.'
Now she was happy, and had some more fun,
And splashed in the water, warmed by the sun.
'Time to go home,' she thought with a sigh,
With a wave to the seashore, she whispered, 'Goodbye.'

The children came home, wanting their tea,
Then Daddy came in and said, 'Save some for me!'
They sat down at the table, already laid,
And tucked into their meal that mummy had made.
While mummy was thinking, with a smile on her face,
'The beach was really nice, but home's the best place.'

Sandra Stoner Mitchell

NOT ALL TOOTH FAIRIES JUST WANT YOUR TEETH

'Come on my dark beauties, there's work to be done!
Rise up from the ground and let's have some fun.'
There's a shuffle and a groan from deep beneath the earth,
A grinning face appears - the tooth fairy's first birth.

'Ah! My first fairy, come, please take flight,
We have children to scare throughout the night.
Don't be afraid of the darkness around,
Let it engulf you as you rise from the ground!'

A second, a third, lots more fairies appear,
A legion of demons with faces to fear,
Toothless and ugly with wings made of bone,
They fly though the air, looking for your home.

Don't try to hide because they'll know where you went,
Their wrinkled noses twitch as they sniff for your scent,
They have grimy little fingers and a manner so uncouth,
Let's hope that under your pillow lies a shiny white tooth.

'So come on my beauties, let me show you the way . . .
If you don't find a tooth, we'll make them pay!
Tug at their ears, and pull hard on their hair,
Make sure that they'll leave you a tooth this time next year.'

Please don't worry children because they might miss your home,
So many houses to choose from and so many places to roam,
But, if you're naughty this year and you think this is funny,
You may not get a good fairy leaving you some money.

J Drake

MISSING OUT

Why does everyone hurry around
With head bent and eyes to the ground?
If only they'd think to look up and see
The regal splendour of the trees.
Tiny white clouds like puffs in the sky
And a myriad of birds all swooping by.
There's more beauty above than can be found
By hurrying around with their eyes to the ground.
It's the same in the city, no one takes the time
To look up and see architecture so fine
All lovingly carved centuries ago
But if no one looks up who's to know?
Maybe if it was the other way round
And all this beauty was on the ground?
Then people being so contraire
Would walk around with their heads in the air!

Maureen Irving

WONDERFUL HANS

Of humble stock and used to poverty,
He grew up in Odense, a cobbler's son,
Well used to stories told, and puppetry,
His childhood yet was not a happy one.
For father died, whose gift he dare not measure,
And he himself so young, his father's treasure.

Twas in his teens he ran away from home
To learn, and for his money beg and plead.
The capital a fitting place to roam,
Wherein he satisfied his youthful greed.
Until his guardians made him school attend,
And all his wanton waywardness to end.

Then, educated well, he chose to write,
And at the outset used a pseudonym.
Thus so, his writing career took gay flight,
And lasting recognition came to him.
For to this day his fairy tales are read,
And many a child goes happily to bed.

Vere Collins

BEING A FAN

At my school some little children,
Some as young as five or six,
Have their fads, their heads are filled then,
With what teacher calls 'idées fixes'

Some collect what football clubs sell,
Posters, shirts and fixture charts:
Girls save dolls like Tinkerbelle,
Pop band photos framed in hearts.

For myself what I was mad on -
Tractors - just you name the marque!
All my bedroom walls I had on
Agriculture bric-a-brac.

On my bed the coverlet
Was a tractor compilation,
Mirrored with another set
On my curtains' combination.

But I've aged, outgrown my habit,
Now I have finesse and poise.
Love of tractors? Not a bit!
Big team football with the boys!

But though I'm eight, I cannot fathom
Why our teacher smirks, (but deadpan)
When in cryptic, mystic wisdom,
Calls me her extractor fan!

P Brady

Yum Yum Treat Land

There is a special land on the far side of the moon,
Climb aboard this jelly rocket, we will be there soon.

Our journey is quick, yes as fast as a snail,
We can get there quicker if we use the lettuce sail.

Now we are landing, I said that we'd be quick,
Hope you enjoyed the ride and not feeling sick.

Gently now be careful as you drop to the ground,
Stay close to me as we go for a look around.

Watch where you tread and mind that treacle slug,
Keep your eyes open for the gingerbread bug.

See over there, how the biscuit bushes grow,
Just behind the custard river in full flow.

Smell spaghetti grass and spy the ginger soil,
Notice the sheep and cows all wrapped in silver foil.

Marvel at liquorice trees, its branches of chocolate chips,
Smothered in leaves made of butter cream whips.

Rows of dolly mixture flowers in blue, green and yellow,
Rich in fluffy pollen made of sticky marshmallow.

Enjoy candyfloss clouds in a lemonade sky,
Come on children hurry there's no time to be shy.

Hear jellybabies gurgle on their strawberry shakes,
If there's time later we'll see the ice cream lakes.

This icing sugar road full of chocice cars,
Look there's a trifle train on a track of toffee bars.

Houses in the valley of sponge and fruit cake,
Over there lolly boats sailing on sugar lakes.

This cherry pie sun so hot and glowing,
Sorry one and all we really must be going.

All aboard the jelly rocket while it's daylight,
Settle down now please and hold on tight.

Take a gift of sweets and lastly I must say,
I promise we'll go back for a longer holiday.

David Watson